Talking with My Father

Talking with My Father

Jesus Teaches on Prayer

Ray C. Stedman

Talking with My Father
Copyright © 1997 by Elaine Stedman

Discovery House Publishers is affiliated with RBC Ministries, Grand Rapids, Michigan 49512

Discovery House books are distributed to the trade exclusively by Barbour Publishing, Inc., Uhrichsville, Ohio 44683

Scripture taken from the Holy Bible, *New International Version.* Copyright © 1973, 1978, 1984 by International Bible Society. Used by permission of Zondervan Publishing House.

Library of Congress Cataloging-in-Publication Data

Stedman, Ray C.
    [Jesus teaches on prayer]
    Talking with my Father : Jesus teaches on prayer / by Ray C. Stedman.
        p.   cm.
    Originally published: Jesus teaches on prayer. Waco, Tex. : Word Books, © 1975.
    ISBN 1-57293-027-6
    1. Jesus Christ—Prayers. I. Title.
BV229.S74 1997
248.3′2—dc21   97-38239
                                              CIP

Printed in the United States of America

99 01 02 00
/ DP /
3 5 7 9 10 8 6 4 2

Contents

Contents

Part One

For Jesus, prayer was as necessary as breathing. If the Son of God felt such a great need for contact with the Father, how much more do we!

But *why?* Why do we need to pray? Certainly God, who knows everything, knows our needs. Why do we need to tell Him what He already knows?

Herein lies one of our most basic misunderstandings about prayer. We think the purpose of prayer is to give information to God: "Lord, I need this and I need that"—as if the Lord didn't already know everything we need!

No, the purpose of prayer is not to inform God about our needs, but to conform us to His will. Prayer doesn't change God. Prayer changes us. It changes our attitude from complaint to praise. It enables us to participate in God's eternal plan. It makes us aware of our total inadequacy—and God's infinite sufficiency.

The goal of faith is to bring us into direct, personal fellowship with God. If we do not move deeper into our fellowship with Him through prayer, we retreat from fellowship with Him. Prayer is active—not static. You cannot stand still in your prayer life. If you don't move forward, you move backward. You either pray your way to a deeper relationship with God—or you lose heart and ultimately give up on faith.

That, as we shall see, is the first thing Jesus teaches us about prayer.

1

Why Pray?

Jesus told his disciples a parable to show them that they should always pray and not give up. He said: "In a certain town there was a judge who neither feared God nor cared about men. And there was a widow in that town who kept coming to him with the plea, 'Grant me justice against my adversary.'

"For some time he refused. But finally he said to himself, 'Even though I don't fear God or care about men, yet because this widow keeps bothering me, I will see that she gets justice, so that she won't eventually wear me out with her coming!' "

And the Lord said, "Listen to what the unjust judge says. And will not God bring about justice for his chosen ones, who cry out to him day and night? Will he keep putting them off? I tell you, he will see that they get justice, and quickly. However, when the Son of Man comes, will he find faith on the earth?"

Luke 18:1–8

When I was in college, I had a roommate who was six feet, seven inches tall, and weighed two-hundred sixty-five pounds. His nickname, of course, was "Tiny." Clearly, this nickname was not intended to *describe* my friend, but to *contrast* with his true description. This common form of contrast is often used to call attention to an outstanding characteristic—for example, when a bald fellow is kiddingly tagged "Curly" or a portly fellow is called "Slim."

Though metaphors and comparisons can often give us a vivid word-picture ("as nervous as a long-tailed cat in a room full of rocking chairs" or "as helpless as a trombone player in a phone booth"), contrast can often be effective in underscoring truth and making it vivid by surprising us. So it is this very form of teaching—the use of surprising contrast—that our Lord employs as He teaches His disciples about prayer in Luke 18:1–8.

Notice the context of Jesus' teaching in this passage: His discussion of prayer immediately follows His prediction of His second coming (this passage in Luke parallels the Lord's Olivet discourse in Matthew 24 and 25). He moves immediately from His words about remaining watchful for His coming to these words about prayer, so He directly links watchfulness and prayer.

The Lord's teaching on prayer in Luke 18 uses three strong contrasts to focus our thinking on prayer. Let's look at those three contrasts as Jesus presents them.

Contrast 1: A Contrast of Principles

Luke clearly and carefully shows us the point Jesus intends to make. Luke says, "Jesus told his disciples a parable to show them that they should always pray and not give up" (Luke 18:1)—or, as other translations put it, "not lose heart," or "not faint." By this Jesus means most simply that we are to pray and not quit. He wants us to be persistent in prayer.

Here Jesus boldly confronts us with a vivid contrast and an inescapable choice: We must either pray or give up, move closer to God or "faint." We must do one or the other. Either we learn to cry out to an unseen Father who is ever present with us, or else we will lose heart.

Some would challenge this principle. "What about people," they ask, "who seem happy without knowing God, without being Christian? They don't pray, yet they seem to enjoy life and experience excitement in their lives. Maybe it is possible to find meaning in life apart from God." Who has not seen such people and wondered if perhaps they have found another alternative, another answer?

Yet when we carefully observe those who seem to have found the secret of life apart from God, those who appear to live in an exciting yet godless world of adventure and romance, we are frequently surprised to find a hidden underside to their lives, a private core of despair that they hide behind a public mask of happiness. Only when they are arrested, check into a drug or alcohol rehab center, or turn up dead of suicide does the public discover the utter emptiness behind the glittering facade.

The list of idols and icons of our society who fit this description is endless: Jack London, Ernest Hemingway, Marilyn Monroe, Mickey Mantle, Jimi Hendrix, Janis Joplin, Jim Morrison of *The Doors*, Elvis Presley, comedian John Belushi, Dennis Wilson of *The Beach Boys*, football player John Matusak, comedian Freddie Prinze, actor River Phoenix, Kurt Cobain of *Nirvana*, model Margaux Hemingway, billionairess Christina Onassis, billionaire heir Amschel Rothschild, and on and on. Outwardly rich, successful, and carefree, they were destroyed by their inner emptiness and despair.

One poignant illustration of this principle is the story of movie mogul Louis B. Mayer, who once ruled MGM studios as if it were his own personal empire. Throughout the 1930s and 1940s, he possessed untold wealth and the incredible power to make and break careers, to control the entertainment choices of a nation, and even to manipulate the Academy Awards presentations. But at the end of his life, as he lay dying of cancer, his last whispered words were, "Nothing matters, nothing matters."

So Jesus was right when He said that only two alternatives exist: Either we pray or we give up. We move deeper into the heart of God—or we lose heart and faint. We are to cry out to Him in prayer, for in Christ His voice has already called to us. We are to answer like a child crying out to his father. For, like children, we do not always know and cannot adequately express what is wrong with us.

Children cannot always express in words what they need or where they hurt, but a loving parent knows. "As a father has compassion on his children, so the LORD has compassion on those who fear him" (Psalm 103:13). When we cry out to God in prayer, we may not understand or articulate our real need, our real hurt—but the Lord knows us through and through. We can depend on Him to hear us, to act on our behalf, to work in our best interests. Even if we do not receive from Him what we want or what we cry out for, we know that we will receive from Him what we *need.*

Here we see the contrast of principles—a contrast between praying and fainting, between going on with God or giving up on God. This is the first contrast Jesus draws for us in this passage on prayer.

Contrast 2: A Contrast of Persons

Next, in Luke 18:1–8, Jesus tells a story that presents a contrast of persons. We see a contrast between the widow and the judge. Who is more weak and defenseless than a widow? And who wields more power over the lives of others than a judge—especially a hard-boiled and unrighteous judge? Here is a tough, self-centered old skinflint, with a heart as cold as the underside of a pillow. In the story, Jesus shows us exactly how harsh he is!

The widow had a persecutor, someone who was harassing her, and she appealed for help. But the judge couldn't care less. He was a godless judge who was utterly unmoved by her pleas, and nothing could reach him. He cared nothing about morality and conscience; he had no regard for persons, so no political pressure could influence him. Clearly, the widow's plight was hopeless.

Nevertheless, explained Jesus, she found a way to get to this unrighteous judge: She made life miserable for him! Day and night, she gave him no rest. She continually made a nuisance of herself before his court, hounding him, harassing him, plaguing him, until finally the judge was forced to act. To get rid of her he granted her request—and she got what she needed!

Here is the point of the story. Jesus says that this widow had found the secret of handling reluctant judges. She had discovered the key to power. She found the one principle on which even a reluctant judge would act, despite his formidable authority. That principle was *persistence.*

So what is Jesus saying? Is He comparing God to an unrighteous judge? No, He is *contrasting* the ungodly, unrighteous judge with the supremely righteous judge over all the universe, God Himself! Here, Jesus gives us a contrast of persons to show us the key to the heart of God, our loving Father. The key to the hard heart of the unrighteous judge was *persistent, perpetual pressure*. The key to the loving heart of God is *persistent, perpetual prayer*.

When we, like the widow, find life to be hopeless and futile, when we fall victim to forces greater than we can manage (and who of us has not been in such a situation?), Jesus says there is still one way out. There is a path to power, there is a solution to our crisis: *prayer*. When we cry out to a God we cannot see but upon whom we may rely, we reach out to a God who possesses a father's heart and a father's compassion. Persistent prayer, says Jesus, always stirs the heart of God. Prayer moves God to action.

Jesus states in no uncertain terms that God is not like the unrighteous judge, that He will not delay in answering our prayers: "And will not God bring about justice for his chosen ones, who cry out to him day and night? Will he keep putting them off?" (Luke 18:7). We do not need to pester God into acting on our behalf. He acts on our behalf because He loves us.

It is sometimes taught that Jesus is encouraging what is called "prevailing prayer"—that is, belaboring and browbeating God into giving us what we want. It's kind of like picketing God, marching up and down, carrying signs, shouting demands, until we finally wear God down. That is an unbiblical and unchristian approach to prayer.

Many years ago, the newspapers carried the story of a Missouri man who announced that he was going on a hunger strike because of the declining moral standards of the nation. He would fast and pray until God sent a great awakening to restore the nation to moral health. He announced that he would continue his fast until he died of starvation or until God acted. Day after day, the newspapers covered the man's fast. His strength began to fail, he grew weaker and weaker, and he was finally confined to his bed. Bulletins regarding his condition were issued each day. Most of us would have quit after the third or fourth day—but not this man. He continued his fast until death. The funeral was widely covered and many lauded his persistence.

But was that truly prayer as God intended? No, it was actually an attempt to *blackmail* God. He held his own life as a pistol to the head of God, demanding that God bend His will to the will of one human being. This man insisted that God act according to a human time schedule. That is not prayer.

Jesus says that God is not an unrighteous God like the judge in the story. He is not grudging or hard-hearted, and we don't have to badger or bully God—nor could we if we wanted to. God hears the prayers of His children, as a father hears the cry of a beloved child, lost and frightened in the dark woods. The child may cry out to be led to an open road, or to be home safe in bed, or at least to see in the distance a light that shows the way to safety. But such prayer is not always answered the way a child demands, because God, our loving Father, already knows what we truly need even before we pray. And He will give us what we *need*, even if He does not always give us what we demand.

Paul reminds us in Romans 12 that we often do not know what to pray for, but God knows. He knows because He is a father, and He also knows when to answer in the particular way we have asked and when that may not be the best thing to do, or even the possible thing to do, under the circumstances.

From our perspective and in terms of what we want, God's answer may seem delayed. But if we could see our lives from a heavenly perspective, we would see that what

Jesus tells us in Luke 18 is true: God's answer to our prayers is not delayed at all.

In 1988, a massive earthquake shook Armenia, collapsing hundreds of buildings and trapping thousands of people in the rubble. Many were rescued from beneath the ruined buildings during the first few hours of the disaster, but after the first day, hope quickly faded that any others would be found alive. One man, however, refused to quit. Why? Because this man was a loving father.

Working feverishly at the ruins of a school where his own son and dozens of other children had been buried by the earthquake, he removed bricks and timbers with his bare hands, working all day and all night. Three days he worked without sleep. Then four days. Then five. People told him to stop, to give up hope. Finally, six days after the quake, he removed a fallen section of wallboard and found an air pocket. He called his son's name—and several young voices weakly answered, including a voice that said, "Daddy, you came for me! I thought you had given up!"

We sometimes think that God takes forever to reach us when we call to Him. Perhaps, at times, it is because our lives are cluttered with so much rubble and debris that He must remove it before we can see the daylight of His love. But He is never slow to respond to our needs. When we cry out in prayer, God answers immediately, instantly, speedily, without delay—and He never gives up. God, our loving Father, never leaves any of His children bereft and alone in a time of need.

God's answer may be the squeeze of His hand on ours, the quiet comfort of a Father's voice, the steady reassurance of a Father's presence even though the woods around us are dark and echoing with fearsome night-sounds. If we listen, we will hear an immediate answering reassurance that the

Father is with us and—in His own time and way—He will lead us home to a place of light and warmth, and He will put us safely, comfortably in our beds. This is what Jesus means when He says, "And will not God bring about justice for his chosen ones, who cry out to him day and night? Will he keep putting them off? I tell you, he will see that they get justice, and quickly" (Luke 18:7–8).

Contrast 3: A Contrast of Practice

Jesus ends His story abruptly with a third contrast—the contrast of practice: "However, when the Son of Man comes, will he find faith on the earth?" (18:8). Notice Jesus does not say, "When the Son of Man comes, He will not find faith on earth," nor does He say, "When the Son of Man comes, He will find faith on earth." He leaves it as an open question, hanging in the air.

But there is no doubt at all about the faithfulness of the Son of Man. He will come. He does not say, *"If* the Son of Man comes," but *"When."* The return of Jesus Christ is an absolute certainty. It does not rest upon humanity, upon human faithfulness or faithlessness. It rests entirely upon the sovereign determination of God. Never doubt that God is ready to do exactly what He says He will do in any circumstances at any time. There is with Him no shadow of turning. The uncertainty is entirely in the latter part of His statement. God is utterly faithful; it is people who are faithful or faltering.

Our Lord's words imply yet another thought: Is it not possible that human beings actually *prefer* weakness over power? Could it be that we actually prefer anxiety over peace, frenzy over rest, doubt over confidence, fear over faith, malice over love? Is it possible that—because of these human tendencies—when the Son of Man comes, He will not find faith on the earth? If our prayers seem to fail, it is not God's fault, it is ours.

Notice something further: Jesus does not ask, "When the Son of Man comes, will He find men praying?" He has been speaking of prayer but now His question is, "When the Son of Man comes, will he find *faith?*" (italics added). Doubtless, the reason for this change is that prayer is the expression of faith. True prayer is not begging or cajoling a reluctant God. True prayer is confidence, trust, and faith in God. Prayer is thanking instead of complaining. Prayer is rejoicing, accepting, appropriating, receiving.

Why Bother to Pray?

"Well," you might say, "if there is a Father out there, and He really knows what we need—why bother to pray?"

The answer to this frequently raised question is that the purpose of prayer is to bring us to an understanding of the Father's heart. Prayer does not always lead us to an answer that satisfies our wants, desires, and curiosities, nor an answer that solves all our problems. But prayer does lead us to a place where we can accept the fact that such answers are unnecessary to accepting and involving ourselves in the vast and mysterious purposes of the Father.

After all, a relationship with God cannot exist without communication. Everyone knows of couples who have stopped speaking to each other. A marriage in which communication has ceased is a marriage in which intimacy and fellowship have disintegrated. That marriage is headed for destruction. Human desires, needs, and feelings must be expressed. There must be an interchange, a flow of ideas and feelings, in order for a marriage relationship to be vital. The same is true of the relationship between ourselves and God.

Prayer is an absolute necessity in the interchange of a child's heart with the Father. This is why Jesus asked, in effect, "When I return, will I find people exercising this blessed privilege? Will I find people expressing themselves to the Father in a warm, living, trusting faith relationship? Will I find people expressing to God the Father all their hurts, joys, complaints, moods, triumphs, failures, and deepest emotions?" That is what a faith relationship with the Father is all about.

A story is told of a father and teenage son who lived in a Spanish village some years ago. One day, they had a terrible argument and both the father and the boy, José, said angry, hurtful things to each other. The son said, "I'm leaving this house, and I don't ever want to speak to you again!" And the father responded, "You won't have to—because you are no longer welcome in this house!" Young José stomped out of the house and was gone.

Years passed. The father regretted the things he had said in that moment of intense emotion. He longed for his son. Finally, the pain of separation became too much for him to bear. He left home and went searching across the length and breadth of Spain—but his son seemed to have disappeared without a trace.

Finally, arriving in the capital city of Madrid, he went to a newspaper office and took out a personal ad in the classified section. It read, "My son, José—I am sorry for the pain I've caused you. Please forgive me. I have forgiven you. I've looked everywhere for you and want only to see you again. I will be at the plaza fountain every day this week at noon. Please meet me there. Your father." It is said that hundreds of young men named José came to the plaza fountain that week, hoping to reestablish a relationship with their fathers.

That is the relationship we all long for, and Jesus has made it possible. That is what prayer is all about—fellowship with the Father. Prayer is the true expression of a living faith relationship. Without prayer, without talking to the Father and listening to Him, what kind of relationship is it? How can we claim to have faith in God while failing to communicate with Him?

One sign of losing communication is that we become obsessed with talk about God. When people only talk *about* God instead of talking *with* God, they demonstrate a deteriorated faith. The purpose of all faith is to bring us into direct, personal touch with God. The mark of a decadent religion is that people become deeply engrossed in discussions about God, spending hours in lengthy, theological debate about the nature and character of God. As Martin Luther aptly put it, "You that manifest a concern about religion, why don't you pray?"

Our goal, as we journey together through the Lord's teaching on prayer, is not that we gain more theological knowledge, but that we experience a deeper faith relationship with the living, true God. So please join with me and pray with me this prayer from the heart:

Our Father, these words of our Lord Jesus have made us aware of the lack of faith in our lives. We cry out to you now in our weakness and our failure for the burning desire to exercise faith and move deeper into a living relationship with you. Father, teach us to pray. Teach us to be men and women who depend continually upon you, who pour out to you every aspect of our lives without hindrance or reservation, who tell you all things, and who listen to you about all things.

In Jesus' name, Amen.

2

The Nature of Prayer

To some who were confident of their own righteousness and looked down on everybody else, Jesus told this parable: "Two men went up to the temple to pray, one a Pharisee and the other a tax collector. The Pharisee stood up and prayed about himself: 'God, I thank you that I am not like other men—robbers, evildoers, adulterers—or even like this tax collector. I fast twice a week and give a tenth of all I get.'

"But the tax collector stood at a distance. He would not even look up to heaven, but beat his breast and said, 'God, have mercy on me, a sinner.'

"I tell you that this man, rather than the other, went home justified before God. For everyone who exalts himself will be humbled, and he who humbles himself will be exalted."

Luke 18:9–14

Louis XIV was king of France during the golden age of French culture, 1643–1715. During his reign, he conducted many foreign conquests that added to the size and power of the French Empire. In 1704, however, Louis launched an attack on the village of Blenheim, Bavaria, and was soundly defeated by English and Austrian forces. Tens of thousands of French soldiers were killed, maimed, or taken prisoner. It was a turning point in the history of France. After that defeat, French military power in Europe steadily declined. When Louis heard about the crushing losses at Blenheim, he raised his hands to heaven and demanded, "God, how could you do this to me after all I have done for you?"

That is the arrogant prayer of a prideful, self-righteous heart. It is a prayer very much like that of the Pharisee, whom Jesus describes in Luke 18:9–14. But like the Pharisee of the Lord's parable, you may say, "I *am* praying. I pray thirty minutes every morning and ten minutes every night, and I am even one of those few who faithfully meet with a midweek prayer group—yet there is still much fainting in my experience. Life is not satisfying to me. I feel I'm not really living."

Or perhaps you are among those who must admit in all honesty that there is very little prayer in your life. For many of us it is hard to pray and easy to find something else to do.

But even if you resolve to try harder to put more prayer into your life, it will not be long before you become aware, as perhaps you already are, that a greater quantity of minutes spent in prayer is not necessarily the answer.

Not *More* Prayer, But *True* Prayer

Is it possible, then, that Jesus is wrong when He says we must either pray or faint? Is prayer such an important issue? Is it possible to pray and faint at the same time? If it seems so, perhaps we need to discover more about the true nature of prayer. It may be that we need a *new kind* of prayer, not just more of the same kind.

True prayer is not a difficult thing. It is natural, instinctive, and comes easily. This kind of prayer is the key to God's power and glory. True prayer is an open channel to God's fatherly compassion and eagerness to help us.

In this parable of Jesus, which could be called "The Parable of the Two Pray-ers," Jesus contrasts two very different men praying two very different prayers from two very different hearts. It is not enough that we simply look at the first pray-er, the Pharisee, and say, "What a proud, self-righteous man!" We must also look at the second pray-er and catch a glimpse of his heart and his motivation in prayer, for he is the Lord's illustration of what true prayer is like.

Notice that the structure of this parable (like the parable of the widow and the unrighteous judge that precedes it, as we saw in chapter 1) is one of contrasts. Our Lord teaches truth by setting it alongside error. By understanding the error of the Pharisee, we can more clearly grasp the truth and reality of the tax collector's prayer.

Now, the Pharisee was a man of prayer—no question about that! He prayed frequently, elaborately, and at great length. His words were loud, lofty, and eloquent. But though he was dedicated to the practice of prayer, the spirit and motivation of his prayer was entirely wrong.

The tax collector, on the other hand, was not accustomed to praying. He was infrequently found in the temple courts. No doubt, his words were halting and lacking in eloquence. This business of praying was all new to him—but his prayer was exactly the right kind of prayer.

In observing the Pharisee, we learn what prayer is not. This kind of praying is not true prayer at all. It's show biz. It's a performance. The Pharisee's focus is not on establishing intimate contact with an infinite God. It is on looking good, on making a good impression. He stood, Jesus said, with his arms spread and his eyes lifted up to heaven. Among the Jews, this was the prescribed posture for prayer.

"The Pharisee stood up," Jesus said, "and prayed about himself" (18:11). Other translations render this last phrase, "and prayed with himself." What a keen thrust that is! The Pharisee was not praying to God—he was praying to himself! No one was at the other end of the line! This prayer was a total waste of time. Many voices in this New-Age-influenced culture of ours falsely claim that the true function of prayer and meditation is to "commune with the inner person." If so, then this Pharisee would fit right into our culture today! When so many people have bought the lie that we are our own gods, then there is no reason to reach any higher in prayer than our own selves.

This Pharisee may have been gazing toward heaven, but he was not reaching toward God—and he certainly was not touching God. Jesus makes this point very clear in His parable.

Who Is a Pharisee?

What do we learn about prayer from the example of the Pharisee? We learn that it is not truly prayer to approach God while we are impressed with our own virtues. This man stood and prayed, "God, I thank you that I am not like other men—robbers, evildoers, adulterers—or even like this tax collector. I fast twice a week and give a tenth of all I get" (18:11–12). He was self-impressed with what he saw as his claims upon God's attention and good favor. He believed that God deserved thanks for having made such a remarkable specimen of humanity as himself!

We laugh as we listen to his foolish prayer, but don't we often do the same? We pray, "Lord, come and help me do this task." In other words, "Lord, I will contribute my ability to exercise leadership, my talents for singing or speaking, and then, Lord, to top it all off, would you give me a little added boost of Spirit-power? Then you and I together will enjoy great success." Our philosophy is frequently, "I do my best and God does the rest." We would never exclude Him and say, "I can do it all." We're much more subtle than that! We simply relegate Him to a supporting role in our accomplishments. I suspect that many, if not most, Christian prayers are prayed from this position.

Sometimes the virtue we contribute to God's program is our "humility." Some Christians demonstrate a kind of reverse brand of Pharisaism that goes something like this: "Thank God, I am not as proud as this Pharisee is." We make ourselves out to be utterly vile, babbling continually about our shortcomings and our sins. We say, "Lord, I am a sinner, I am a louse, I'm no good." At some level, we think we can impress God with our show of "humility." In reality, we have invested self-righteous, pharisaic pride in our "humility," which is not humility at all!

The simple truth is that we have no virtues of our own to contribute, none whatsoever. We have absolutely nothing to add to God's cause. We must forget all our talents, abilities, skills, gifts, and accomplishments. Those things all come from God, not from us. They are not our possessions, but merely on loan from Him.

Isn't it strange how easily we identify ourselves with our virtues—and how quickly we excuse our faults? Our failures we blame on everyone else; for our successes we take full credit. How many times have we heard public figures who are caught up in scandal say, "Mistakes were made," or, "I was a victim of poor judgment," instead of, "I have sinned," or, "I have committed a crime," or, "I alone am at fault." Unlike the humble tax collector's confession, "Mistakes were made" is not an admission of wrongdoing, but an attempt to excuse or cover up wrongdoing, in the proud, self-righteous tradition of the Pharisee. And if we are honest with ourselves and with God, we all have to admit that we are guilty of doing the same, time after time, in our own lives.

We easily forget our own failings and faults when we compare ourselves with others. We forget our clever manipulations, our lusts and evil thoughts, our deliberate deceits, our phony sympathies, our dubious business arrangements. We are careful to remember only our virtues. How do we become so impressed with ourselves? Like this Pharisee, we look downward. When he looked down on the tax collector, he immediately felt prideful regarding his own supposed "virtue." So he thanked the Lord that he was not like that vile, low-down tax collector.

This is the point Jesus makes in describing the Pharisee. He says in effect that when we approach God on this level, we are praying with ourselves. This is not true prayer. Our pious words, our properly phrased sentences, our completely orthodox approach is of no value whatever. We are praying out of an obsession with our own virtues.

Furthermore, Jesus says it is not prayer when we ask God's help because of our own accomplishments. This Pharisee said he fasted twice a week—much more than was required by the law, which commanded a fast only once a year. He gave tithes of all he got; again, that was more than the law required. But the Pharisee expected God to act on his behalf because he felt God could hardly do otherwise in view of his fine record of faithful service.

It's Not Fair!

Many years ago, an elderly missionary couple returned from Africa to retire in New York City. As their ship steamed into New York harbor, they reflected on their bleak situation: They had no pension, for they belonged to no missionary board. Their health was broken. They were defeated, discouraged, and fearful about the future. And they couldn't help comparing their circumstances with those of a fellow passenger who also had boarded the ship in Africa—President Teddy Roosevelt, who was returning from one of his big-game hunting expeditions.

As the ship pulled into the harbor, past the great city and the Statue of Liberty, the people on the ship could hear a band playing on the dock. A huge crowd had gathered to welcome the returning president from his hunting trip in Africa. The old missionary turned and said to his wife, "Dear, something is wrong. Why should we have given our lives in faithful service for God in Africa all these years? This man comes back from a big-game hunting expedition and everybody makes a big fuss over him, but nobody gives two hoots about us."

"Dear," his wife replied, "you shouldn't feel that way. Try not to be bitter about it."

"I just can't help it," he replied. "It's not right. After all, if God is running this world, why does He permit such injustice?" As the boat neared the dock, as the sound of the band and the cheering of the crowd grew louder, he became more and more depressed.

The mayor of New York City was on hand to greet the returning president, along with many other dignitaries—but no one even noticed the missionary couple. They slipped off the ship and found a cheap flat on the east side, hoping the next day to see what they could do to make a living in the city.

That night the man's spirit just broke. He said to his wife, "I can't take this! God is not fair! We don't even know anyone to help us, or where to go. If God is faithful, why doesn't He meet our need?"

"Why don't you ask Him?" said his wife.

"All right," said the man. "I will." He went into the bedroom and prayed for a while. Later, when he emerged from the bedroom after talking it over with God, he seemed completely changed.

"Dear, what happened?" asked his wife. "What has come over you?"

"Well," he said, "the Lord settled it with me. I went in and knelt beside the bed and poured out my feelings to Him. I said, 'Lord, it's not fair!' I told Him how bitter I was that the president should receive this tremendous homecoming, when no one met us as we returned home. And when I finished, it seemed as though the Lord put His hand on my shoulder and simply said, 'But you're not home yet!' "

That's a great truth, isn't it? God does reward believers, but not necessarily down here. The rewards here have to do with the strengthening of the inner life, not the outer. We have no claim on God by reason of our faithful service. Serving Him is only what we should do. We have no right to come to Him in prayer and demand that He answer because we have done this, that, or another thing.

Jesus says that when we stand and list our accomplishments before God, we are not praying. Is it any wonder then that we have been fainting? Is it possible that after years of praying we must now realize we have never truly prayed?

Upside-Down Is All Right

Now let's examine the tax collector's prayer.

It seems at first that he does it all wrong: He stands at a distance. He doesn't even lift up his eyes—he fails to assume the proper position of prayer. But how totally unimportant are these external issues.

A poem by Sam Walter Foss, "The Prayer of Cyrus Brown," says it so well:

> "The proper way for a man to pray,"
> Said Deacon Lemuel Keyes,
> "And the only proper attitude
> Is down upon his knees."
>
> "No, I should say the way to pray,"
> Said Reverend Doctor Wise,
> "Is standing straight with outstretched arms
> And rapt and upturned eyes."
>
> "Oh, no, no, no," said Elder Slow,
> "Such posture is too proud.
> A man should pray with eyes fast-closed
> And head contritely bowed."
>
> "It seems to me his hands should be
> Austerely clasped in front
> With both thumbs pointing toward the ground,"
> Said Reverend Doctor Blunt.
>
> "Last year I fell in Hidgekin's well
> Headfirst," said Cyrus Brown,
> "With both my heels a-stickin' up
> And my head a-pointin' down.

"And I made a prayer right then and there,
The best prayer I ever said,
The prayingest prayer I ever prayed,
A-standin' on my head."

The tax collector would have identified well with ol' Cyrus Brown. He understood that what God wanted was not elegant speech or a certain posture. God was interested in the sincerity and earnestness of the tax collector's heart. So the man came into the temple and stood with his eyes cast down. All he could do was beat his breast and say, "God be merciful to me a sinner."

Someone has called the tax collector's prayer "a holy telegram." I like that description: A short, pithy, right-to-the-point prayer. Most of all, a *true* prayer, genuine and from the heart.

What do we learn about prayer from this man? Isn't it obvious that authentic prayer, the most profound prayer, is the expression to God of our helpless need? The tax collector saw himself as the lowest form of life on earth—a miserable, helpless sinner. The original language makes it clear that he is talking about the very lowest, worst kind of sinner. This man believed he deserved nothing from God, and without God he could do absolutely nothing to help his position: "I'm a sinner, Lord, that's all I can say; I have nothing else to add."

The tax collector rests his entire case on the merciful character of God, nothing on his own merit. He says, in effect, "Lord, I haven't a thing to lean on but you." Yes, he wanted to change his ways and live a repentant, honest, holy life before God—but not to gain God's favor. No, he wanted to change his ways as a response of gratitude and thanks to God's mercy.

He needed God. He had to have God. And so he came in complete humility and cast himself down on God's altar of mercy.

Judge Upward

IIow did the tax collector come to this place of repentant prayer? In exactly the opposite direction as the Pharisee. The Pharisee looked down on those around him. The tax collector looked up to God. The Pharisee judged downward, comparing himself with unholy men. The tax collector judged upward, comparing himself with a holy, righteous God. The Pharisee prayed with himself. The tax collector saw no one and prayed to no one but God. He had heard the words of Scripture, "Love the Lord your God with all your heart and with all your soul and with all your mind" (Matthew 22:37; compare Mark 12:30, Luke 10:27), and judged himself on that basis: "Lord, I'm a sinner! I need mercy!" And by praying that abject, humble prayer for mercy, without excuses or evasions, everything that God is suddenly became available to the tax collector.

We will never find answers to the awesome problems that afflict us individually and as a society—juvenile delinquency, rampant adultery and immorality, broken families, pornography, teen pregnancy, drug and alcohol addiction, gossip and back-stabbing, scandal, abuse, and on and on—until each of us casts ourselves wholly upon God and cries out, "Lord, I'm a sinner! I need mercy!"

Unfortunately, we seem to think that such a confession is "for emergency use only." We cast ourselves upon God's mercy only when our backs are against the wall and we have nowhere else to turn. Instead, this should be our normal, everyday basis of living—the fact that we are helpless to save ourselves, that there is no righteousness in us, that we are sinners in need of mercy, beggars deserving nothing, without excuse before God. True prayer, then, is an expression of our helplessness, an awareness of need that only God can meet.

But the tax collector's prayer not only shows us our own inadequacy as sinful human beings—it highlights the reality of God's complete adequacy as the righteous Lord of creation. The tax collector said, "God, be merciful to me," and this is true prayer.

In that word *merciful* is hidden the entire, wonderful story of the coming of Jesus Christ, His lowly birth in Bethlehem, His amazing ministry on earth, the bloody cross, the empty tomb. In this prayer, when the tax collector begs God to be merciful, he uses a special word in the original Greek, a theological word that means "be propitiated to me." In other words, he is saying to God, "Having had your justice satisfied, Lord, now show me your love." And he believed that God's mercy was his, for Jesus said that this man went back to his house justified. He was changed; he was different; he was made whole. He claimed what God had promised—and that, too, is true prayer: Trusting, taking, claiming God's promises.

Genuine prayer is more than asking; prayer is taking. Genuine prayer is more than pleading; prayer is believing. Genuine prayer is more than words uttered; prayer is an attitude maintained. How many times we ought to be praying! Whenever there is an awareness of need, that is an opportunity to let the heart, the thought, and the voice (whatever form prayer may take) lift immediately to God and say, "God, be merciful. Lord, meet this need. My hope, my help, my everything is in you for this moment." It doesn't matter whether it is only tying your shoes or washing the dishes or writing a letter or writing a term paper or making a telephone call. Whenever there's a need, that is the time for prayer. Prayer is an expression of dependence that uses God's resources for any need in our lives.

Now, the question I ask of my own heart is this: Have I ever *truly* prayed? If what Jesus says is true—that prayer is the opposite of fainting—then why do I find my life so often filled with fainting, losing heart, discouragement, and defeat? The obvious answer is that I have not been truly praying, for true prayer and fainting, true prayer and defeat, cannot exist together.

Have you ever prayed? Have you ever *truly* prayed? Has your prayer life been like that of the Pharisee or like that of the tax collector? Have you ever launched upon a life of prayer where every moment you are counting on God to meet your need? Will you, this day, begin that life?

Perhaps today, for the first time in your life, you can say, "Lord, be merciful to me, a sinner." That is the true nature of prayer.

Holy Father, help us to take these examples of prayer seriously—both the example of the Pharisee and the example of the tax collector. The stories of Jesus are not intended merely to entertain us or even to instruct us, but to change us, to set us free, to enable us to live, to turn us from weakness and emptiness and barrenness, to truth and life and joy. We ask now that we may begin to live a life of authentic prayer, of authentic fellowship with you. We have no other help, no other adequacy. You alone are fully adequate. On this we rest.

In Jesus' name, Amen.

3

How Jesus Prayed

One day Jesus was praying in a certain place. When he finished, one of his disciples said to him, "Lord, teach us to pray, just as John taught his disciples."

Luke 11:1

Jesus was a source of continual amazement to His own disciples. Life with Him was one unending experience of alternating joy and bewilderment, and they were forever attempting to explain Him to their own satisfaction.

The disciples had traveled with Jesus the length and breadth of the land of Israel, and it had been like a great military campaign. They saw inroads made into the dark powers of sickness, death, and despair throughout the land. They could not forget the mighty demonstrations of His power. They remembered the grateful eyes of the lame, blind, sick, dumb, and deaf—the afflicted who had been healed and set free and sent back to their loved ones. They were continually astonished at the wisdom Jesus manifested, and were forever watching Him, seeking to discover the secret of His wisdom and power. All the time He was eating, sleeping, teaching, traveling, they were watching.

In Luke 11:1 we read that Jesus was praying, and when He finished, one of the disciples, speaking for all the disciples, said, "Lord, teach us to pray." This is a significant request, because these disciples undoubtedly were already men of prayer. When this one said to Him, "Lord, teach us to pray, as John taught his disciples," he did not mean that John had a superior school of ministry. He was not saying, "In that traveling seminary that John conducted, he had a course on prayer—but you have not told us anything about this yet." What he meant was, "Some of us once were John's disciples and were taught by him how to pray. But Lord, we have been watching you and we see that you are a master at prayer. Now, as John once taught us how to pray, would you also impart to us the secrets of prayer? We can see that, in some way, the marvel and mystery of your character is linked with your prayer life, and it has made us aware of how little we really know about prayer. Lord, would you teach us to pray?"

My heart's deepest desire is that in all simplicity and in an awareness of our deep need, we each might cry out as did this disciple, "Lord, teach us to pray." For the brutal fact is that we do not know how to pray, either as individuals or as a church. And the proof that we do not know how to pray as individuals is found in the tremendous amount of fainting that is visible in our midst—the discouragement, anxiety, fear, guilt, and despair that is evident in many lives.

People who are familiar with the strengthening ministry of prayer in their individual lives have an undeniable joy and glow that is wonderful to see. They can approach every circumstance with that compelling air of triumph that marks the authentic Christian faith, and in their lives the ministry of prayer is very evident. But we must admit there is much fainting, too, among young and old alike, and this marks the lack of real prayer.

If we who are Christians fail in this vital area, it is simply because we have not yet seen what prayer is or understood what part it plays in Christian living. Somehow the enemy has blurred our senses and dimmed our eyes so that we do not see this clearly.

Prayer, as we have seen in previous chapters, is simply the expression of human need to an eager, loving Father. It is the cry of a beloved child to a Father who is ready to pour out all that He has to give. As we join this unnamed disciple, and cry out to God from the depths of our desperate, needy lives, "Lord, teach us to pray," one thing becomes immediately evident: By saying these words from our hearts, we take the first and most important step toward discovering the power of prayer.

The Breath of Life

What was it that so impressed the disciples as they watched Jesus pray? What convinced them that His prayer life and His amazing power and wisdom were somehow related?

They saw, first of all, that with Jesus prayer was a necessity. It was more than an occasional practice on His part; it was a lifelong habit. It was an attitude of mind and heart—an atmosphere in which He lived, the very air He breathed. Everything He did arose out of prayer. He literally prayed without ceasing, as the apostle Paul urges us to do.

Obviously, it was not always formal prayer. He did not always kneel or continually stand with bowed head in an attitude of prayer. If He had, of course, He wouldn't have been able to do anything else!

And it is amazing that He fulfilled His prayer life in the midst of an incredibly busy ministry. Just imagine how much ministry He crammed into three short years! He was subjected, like many of us, to a life of increasing pressure, of continual interruption. As He ministered, He met with growing opposition, with increasing harassment and continual resistance to the course He was taking, even from His own disciples. Yet in the midst of this life of incredible busyness and tremendous pressure and frequent interruption, He was constantly in prayer.

Prayer is often the first thing squeezed out of our busy schedules. We often excuse ourselves for our prayerlessness by saying, "I've got so much to do today, I don't have time to pray!" But one of the founders of the Protestant Reformation, Martin Luther, looked at prayer another way. He was often heard to say, "I have so much to do today, I need to spend an extra hour in prayer!" It is amazing but true: Taking time to pray often adds time to our day.

Spending quality time with God, talking to Him and listening for His response, helps us center our thoughts and prioritize our tasks. Who better to consult for time management advice than the One who created time?

Certainly, that is the example set for us by the Lord Jesus. He was praying in spirit when His hands were busy healing. He gave thanks as He broke the bread and fed the five thousand. He gave thanks to the Father at the tomb of Lazarus before He spoke those words, "Lazarus, come out!" (John 11:43), in that dramatic display of power. When the Greeks came and wanted to see Jesus, His immediate response was one of prayer: "Father, glorify your name!" (John 12:28). There was a continual sense of expectation that the Father would be working through Him, and thus, by His very attitude, Jesus was praying all the time.

Here we find the secret of prayer and of the effective prayer life: *Practice an attitude of constant expectancy.* When we do that, we are never very far from the thought that God is working in us and through us to perform His will and complete His plan. Jesus did this, of course, because He believed and practiced what He preached. He said continually, "I tell you the truth, the Son can do nothing by himself; he can do only what he sees his Father doing, because whatever the Father does the Son also does" (John 5:19). Those were not mere pious phrases. He was not simply trying to make a good impression on those around Him. He was saying something that startled them—but He meant it with every fiber of His being. "The Son can do nothing by himself"—what an amazing thing for Him to say!

Here is the Son of God Himself—the perfect man, the One who adequately and continually fulfilled God's expectation for humanity, the One who was the constant delight of the Father's heart, the One who was fully God and fully man. Yet He tells us that He did nothing—absolutely nothing—by Himself. Again and again, He declared His utter dependency on the Father: "Don't you believe that I am in the Father, and that the Father is in me? The words I say to you are not just my own. Rather, it is the Father, living in me, who is doing his work" (John 14:10).

Out of this constant, conscious sense of His own need for connection with—and dependence on—the Father arose a continuing attitude of prayer, a continuing expectation that if anything was to be done, the Father would have to do it. The Son of Man did nothing by Himself.

For Emergency Use Only?

John G. Paton and his wife, a missionary couple in the New Hebrides Islands, had an absolutely astounding experience with prayer. One night, some years ago, they found their mission headquarters surrounded by hostile tribespeople. The islanders carried torches, and their plan was to burn down the headquarters with Mr. and Mrs. Paton inside. The missionary couple prayed to God throughout the night. At dawn, they looked outside and saw that the tribespeople had gone. Surprised but grateful, the Patons went to their knees and thanked God for their mysterious deliverance.

Some time later, the chief of the tribe was converted to faith in Jesus Christ. Mr. Paton asked the new Christian about that night, when he and his people had come to burn down the mission headquarters. "Why," asked Paton, "didn't you kill us that night?"

"We tried to," said the chief, "but we couldn't. The men who guarded your house wouldn't let us near."

Baffled, the missionary said, "What men? We had no men guarding the house. There was no one in or around that house but my wife and me."

"We know what we saw," said the chief. "We saw warriors standing guard—tall men in shining robes, with fiery swords in their hands. When we tried to attack, they held us off. They surrounded the mission house so we could not get to it."

So Mr. Paton and his wife have very good reason to believe in God, in angels, and in the power of prayer—especially in an emergency!

Unfortunately, a lot of people think prayer is *only* for emergencies. They operate by the saying, "If all else fails—pray." If we are honest with ourselves, we have to admit that this has been our own attitude many times. Our problem is one of self-sufficiency. When everything is going well, when we are successful and comfortable, when the road ahead is smooth, we think, "I'm doing fine all by myself. Who needs God?" Oh, we would never express such a thought aloud, but that's what our self-sufficient attitude really comes down to.

Then trouble strikes—a difficult relationship, a stressful time on the job, a financial reversal, a catastrophic accident, a serious illness—and suddenly we are intensely aware of our inadequacy and our need. Suddenly, we are ready for prayer. Why do we so often wait until trouble strikes before we go to God in prayer? Why do we so often think of prayer as "For Emergency Use Only"?

But the secret of Jesus' life was that prayer, for Him, was never a last resort. It was His first resort! A lifestyle of prayer maintained Him through the easy times and sustained Him through the hard times. He didn't depend on God to get Him through only life's tough times. He continually depended on God. His entire life was derived from God. His constant attitude was, "The Son can do nothing by Himself."

That must be our attitude as well. Prayer is not for emergencies only. Our entire lives should be lived in absolute dependence on God through prayer.

The Fishing Expert

On one occasion, our Lord addressed a great crowd on the lakeshore. As He spoke, the people pressed so closely He could no longer be easily seen or heard (see Luke 5:1–8). So He climbed into Peter's boat and told him to move out a bit into the lake. Peter rowed the boat a few yards from shore, so the Lord could be seen and heard much better. Jesus continued His sermon.

Imagine how Peter must have felt! At last he was able to do something for his Lord. It was his boat, and the Lord was his guest. The Lord had done so much for him that his heart must have rejoiced at this opportunity to provide something that Christ needed and without which He could not have carried on His ministry that day. But when our Lord finished His discourse and dismissed the crowd, He turned and said, "Peter, move the boat out into the deep part of the lake." When Peter had taken the boat out into the middle of the lake, the Lord said, "Now, Peter, cast in your net. Get ready to fish."

Peter looked at the Lord in amazement. You can almost see the incredulous look on his face and hear the patronizing tone in his voice when he replied, "Lord, we have been fishing all night long and caught nothing!" He was undoubtedly thinking, "Lord, I know you are a great teacher. You obviously know secrets that we know nothing about. But Lord, when it comes to fishing, I'm the expert. If you want to know anything about fishing, I'll be glad to instruct you. After all, Lord, I have been raised on this lake. I know where fish are and where they aren't.

Take my advice, Lord—you stick to preaching, and I'll do the fishing."

But the Lord said, "Peter, let down your nets for a catch."

Something about His tone was so irresistible that Peter replied, in effect, "All right, Lord, I think it's crazy, but if you say so, I'll do it." So Peter let down the net and enclosed a great host of fish so large that the nets began to break as they drew the fish into the boat. Peter dumped the fish into the bottom of the boat, then fell to his knees and looked up at his Lord in amazement. "Go away from me, Lord," he said. "I am a sinful man!"

What did Peter mean? He meant, "Lord, I see what you mean. I see that, even in those areas where I think I'm sufficient, I need you."

Surely this is what our Lord wants to teach us. This is one thing we must learn: every activity of life requires prayer, a sense of expectation of God at work. Is not this what that disciple felt (it may even have been Peter) as he watched our Lord praying? The disciple knew that, to him, prayer was an option. He prayed when he felt like it, only when he considered it necessary; he believed that prayer was designed for emergency use only, for the "big" problems of life. But he saw that, for Jesus, prayer was an ever-present necessity.

Where do we begin to acquire this Christlike need for prayer, this Christlike dependency on prayer? We need to begin right where we are. You begin with that phone call you are about to make—you can't do it right except by prayer. Before you pick up the phone, look to God and say, "Lord, speak through me during this phone call."

You begin with the letter you are about to write. The component you are attaching on the assembly line. The meeting you are about to attend. The interview you are about to conduct. The game you are about to play with your children. The homework you are about to begin. The report you must write for the boss. The room you are sweeping. The walk you are going to take. The drive to the store you are about to begin. The class you are about to teach. These are the unending needs from which prayer rises. You begin to acquire a Christlike prayer life when you approach every activity of your life saying, "Lord, I can't do anything apart from you. Father, please do this thing through me."

Someone once asked a dear cleaning lady what her method of prayer was, and she said, "I don't know nothin' about method. I just pray like this: When I wash my clothes, I pray, 'Lord, wash my heart clean.' When I iron them I say, 'Lord, iron out all these troubles I can't do nothin' about.' When I sweep the floor, I say, 'Lord, sweep all the corners of my life like I'm sweepin' this floor.' " That is real prayer.

Necessary—and Natural

The second thing the disciples saw in Jesus was that prayer was not only necessary but it was also perfectly natural. Jesus did not struggle, strive, or drive Himself to pray. Prayer was not an act of self-discipline or duty—it was always His delight.

That doesn't mean our Lord did not have to make time and even schedule time for prayer—He needed to, just as we need to. He had to make choices between prayer and other demands on His time—just as we do. Sometimes He spent hours and even entire nights in prayer. Occasionally He slipped away when the crowds grew large and demanding—times when most of us might be tempted to cut back on our prayer time in order to meet those demands. In Luke 5:16, for example, a great multitude came to hear Him, but He withdrew to a desert place and prayed.

Certainly, Jesus experienced times of extreme weariness, times when praying was very difficult. The night He prayed in Gethsemane—the same night His disciples were overcome by exhaustion and sleep—He fought emotional and physical exhaustion and spent those dark hours in the presence of the Father. Scripture records no reluctance in His approach to prayer, no sense that He had to drag Himself away from something else in order to pray.

Why not? Because His actions arose from an overwhelming sense of need. He craved a daily, even hourly relationship with the Father—and He knew that, whatever else might be on His agenda for the day, time spent in prayer is never wasted. He knew that hours of activity without prayer would accomplish nothing. The Lord felt a continuous, urgent sense of need, an awareness that He was but an empty channel or vessel through whom the Father worked—and it was out of this awareness that His prayer life arose.

And this is what it must come to for you and me. We urgently require a sense of need! Offer a sandwich to a man who has just eaten a heavy dinner and you will have to use all your powers of persuasion to get him to accept it. If he does, it will only be out of politeness, and as soon as your back is turned he will dispose of it behind the sofa. Why? Because he has no sense of need. Though he may feel a duty to accept it, he does not want it, and it is of no value to him. But offer that same sandwich to a hungry teenage boy—and you'd better head for the kitchen to make more sandwiches before he finishes the first!

To Jesus, prayer was as necessary as eating—and just as natural.

Just Talking to My Father

Prayer, for Jesus, often meant thanksgiving. We see such a prayer of thanksgiving in Luke 10:

> At that time Jesus, full of joy through the Holy Spirit, said, "I praise you, Father, Lord of heaven and earth, because you have hidden these things from the wise and learned, and revealed them to little children. Yes, Father, for this was your good pleasure.
>
> "All things have been committed to me by my Father. No one knows who the Son is except the Father, and no one knows who the Father is except the Son and those to whom the Son chooses to reveal him" (Luke 10:21–22).

Jesus was always giving thanks. He was forever saying, "Thank you, Father. Thank you for the circumstance into which you have brought me, thank you for the victory that will be won through these circumstances, thank you for the needs that are being met." As He broke the bread to feed the five thousand, He lifted His eyes and said, "Thank You, Father." At the Last Supper, as He gathered with His own in the Upper Room, He took the cup and when He had given thanks, He said, "Take, eat." Throughout Jesus' life, He prayed His thanks to God.

Jesus sometimes prayed for counsel from His Father. On the occasion when He was about to choose His disciples, He spent all the previous night in prayer (see Luke 6:12–13). What was He doing? He was seeking and receiving illumination and guidance from the Father. He knew His own wisdom would be inadequate for this task. He went into the presence of the Father and together they went down the list of prospective disciples and talked over every single one. As He talked with the Father about each of them, a conviction came to His heart. When He had finished, He'd chosen the Twelve, including Judas.

For Jesus, prayer was also frequently intercession. We have a matchless example of it in John 17—that mighty prayer in which He prayed for the eleven apostles and through them for the whole church to every succeeding age. "My prayer is not for them alone. I pray also for those who will believe in me through their message" (17:20). He prayed for Peter in the hour of his disillusionment and defeat when his world came crashing around his head in the dark night that he denied his Lord. The Lord had met him (using his old name, Simon) before and said, "Simon, Simon, Satan has asked to sift you as wheat. But I have prayed for you, Simon, that your faith may not fail. And when you have turned back, strengthen your brothers" (Luke 22:31–32). Both Judas and Peter denied their Lord that night, but one of the fundamental differences between Judas and Peter was that Christ had prayed for Peter.

He prayed for the little children and made intercession for them with the Father. And finally, His great prayer of intercession was prayed on the bloody cross. He prayed as they hammered the nails into the flesh of His outstretched arms, "Father, forgive them, for they do not know what they are doing" (Luke 23:34).

But above all else, prayer, to Jesus, was communion. He prayed on the Mount of Transfiguration, and as His disciples watched, He was suddenly transformed before them. The appearance of His face was altered and His garments became white and shining. In prayer, He experienced a communion so rich that the glory of the Father, the indwelling glory broke through the tent of His body in which it was hidden. As John 1:14 tells us, "We have seen his glory, the glory of the One and Only, who came from the Father, full of grace and truth."

Jesus prayed in the Garden and experienced real communion in an hour of deep anguish of heart. As He prayed, He was strengthened by an angel who ministered to Him in the midst of the pressures He faced. So, as we trace the prayer life of Jesus, we can see that prayer was necessary and natural to Him.

Why, then, do we struggle so with prayer?

Who Said That?

We often find ourselves very busy when it's time for prayer meeting. We piously favor prayer in general—yet resist prayer at those specific times when the opportunity or need for prayer arises. If we reflect on what runs through our minds at such times, we may detect the subtle whispers of the enemy, Satan, whispering two very clever and destructive messages to us about prayer.

One message: "Of course Jesus prayed continually, easily, naturally—what do you expect? He's the Son of God, after all! Certainly, *you* don't expect to live and pray on the same level as *Him*, do you? Isn't it obvious that a Christlike prayer life is far beyond your capacity? After all, you are nothing but a simple, ordinary Christian."

Like everything else the devil says to us, that is a filthy, destructive lie. The Lord Jesus tells us, "Just as the living Father sent me and I live because of the Father, so the one who feeds on me will live because of me" (John 6:57). As He lived by the Father's strength, so we are to live by the Son's strength in exactly the same relationship.

The second message: "Well, Jesus prayed as He did because He felt a sense of need continually. It is easy to pray, you know, when you feel need. So go ahead and pray when you need to. But don't bother unless you feel you have to." That is just more satanic mind-slime! It's a restatement of the current, widespread philosophy: Follow your feelings. In other words, don't bother to walk by faith.

Faith rests on fact, and the fact God reveals to us is that, whether or not we sense a need, we are needy. Whether we feel sufficient or not, we are insufficient. We are continually needy and we must constantly depend upon the indwelling life and strength of the Lord Jesus. When we think everything is fine and under control, and we need no help from God, we are suffering from a satanic delusion. It's nothing more than a soap bubble of imagination, destined to burst in slippery confusion.

Life is under control *only* when our attitude is what Jesus' attitude was: one of continual need and constant expectation. God is always the same, and our faith must continually rest on that great unshakable Rock, and nothing else. It is His job to give power and strength—and our job to receive. Prayer is to be our life and our breath. We should need no more urging to pray than we need urging to eat and breathe! We know we must pray.

Once, when I stood at the Lincoln Memorial in Washington, D.C., I read again those amazing words engraved on the walls—Lincoln's Gettysburg Address and his Second Inaugural Address. The words of the latter came home to me with tremendous impact. It is more like a sermon than a political speech. I remembered that when Lincoln entered the presidency he was not a Christian, as he himself has said. But as the burdens of that great office devolved upon him and the crushing responsibility and sorrow of the war gripped his heart, he said that while he was walking among the graves of the soldiers at Gettysburg, there burst upon him an awareness of his need of the Savior. That is where he became a Christian.

In the terrible crucible of the Civil War, Lincoln learned to pray. For him, the purpose of prayer was not to get God to do man's bidding, but to enable man to see God's purposes and to experience the strength of relying on the everlasting arms. Lincoln left this testimony about prayer: "I have been driven many times to my knees by the overwhelming conviction that I had absolutely no other place to go." In the strength of that continual reliance upon God, he became our nation's greatest president.

Will it take a crucible of testing to drive you to your knees in prayer? Or will you follow the example of your Lord, learning to pray as continuously and naturally as breathing, in the good times and the hard times? My prayer for you is that you make a commitment today, at this very moment, to make your everyday life a life of prayer.

Father, what can we say in this hour but to cry out as these disciples cried out, "Lord, teach us to pray." Teach us our need. Tear away this veil from our eyes that makes us think we have any adequacy in ourselves. Deliver us from this satanic delusion, this widespread worldly philosophy that our knowledge, our education, our training can provide an adequate background for activity. Give us instead a conscious sense of dependence on you, an awareness that nothing we do will have any lasting value apart from daily, hourly, intimate communion with you.

In Jesus' name, Amen.

4

The Pattern of Prayer

One day Jesus was praying in a certain place. When he finished, one of his disciples said to him, "Lord, teach us to pray, just as John taught his disciples."

He said to them, "When you pray, say:

" 'Father, hallowed be your name, your kingdom come. Give us each day our daily bread. Forgive us our sins, for we also forgive everyone who sins against us. And lead us not into temptation.' "

Luke 11:1–4

A true story:

During the 1950s, when Hollywood produced some of its most famous biblical epics (such as *The Robe, Ben Hur,* and *The Ten Commandments),* a couple of movie studio executives were discussing the possibility of producing a biblical epic for their studio. One asked the other, "What do you know about the Bible? I'll bet you fifty bucks you don't even know the Lord's Prayer."

"I do so," said the other. "Listen: 'Now I lay me down to sleep. . . .' "

The first exec sighed, pulled out his wallet, and handed the other man fifty dollars. "Amazing," he said. "Where did you learn so much about the Bible?"

One shudders to think of the movie that emerged when these two Hollywood producers pooled their biblical ignorance! Jesus has given us His pattern for prayer—and that pattern does *not* begin with the words, "Now I lay me down to sleep"!

Last chapter we observed the prayer life of our Lord Jesus in Luke 11:1 through the eyes of an unnamed disciple who watched Him pray. As we looked together at Jesus' prayer life, I hope a dawning conviction stole over you, as it did over this unnamed disciple: Prayer was the secret of the Lord's amazing life, and it was both the most natural and most necessary aspect of His existence. I hope, too, that you heard within yourself the urgent cry of this disciple, "Lord, teach us to pray."

In answer to this request, Jesus gave His disciples what is called the model prayer, the Lord's Prayer. We have a very brief account of it in Luke 11:

He said to them, "When you pray, say: 'Father, hallowed be your name, your kingdom come. Give us each day our daily bread. Forgive us our sins, for we also forgive everyone who sins against us. And lead us not into temptation' " (Luke 11:2–4).

This is slightly different from the more familiar form in Matthew which was undoubtedly spoken on a different occasion (Jesus frequently repeated the great truths He taught during His ministry):

> "This, then, is how you should pray:
> " 'Our Father in heaven, hallowed be your name, your kingdom come, your will be done on earth as it is in heaven. Give us today our daily bread. Forgive us our debts, as we also have forgiven our debtors. And lead us not into temptation, but deliver us from the evil one' " (Matthew 6:9–13).

This prayer falls into two rather obvious divisions, highlighted by the use of two pronouns. The first part centers on God, using the pronoun *your.* "Hallowed be your name, your kingdom come." The second part concerns humanity, and here we see the pronoun *us.* "Give us today our daily bread. Forgive us our debts, as we also have forgiven our debtors. And lead us not into temptation." For now, we will confine ourselves to those first three phrases that center around the person, character, and being of God.

Begin with God

It is no accident, I am sure, that in prayer as in everything else, Jesus invariably puts God first. Surely this exposes a fatal weakness in our own prayers, which so frequently begin with us. We rush almost immediately into a series of pleading petitions that have to do with *our* problems and *our* needs and *our* irritations. This only serves to focus our attention on what is already troubling us and to increase our awareness of our lack. Perhaps that is the reason we frequently end up more depressed or more frustrated than when we began.

But Jesus shows us another way. He begins with God. Jesus' example shows that we must take a slow, calm, reassuring gaze at the Father—at His greatness and His eagerness to give, His unwearied patience and untiring love. Then, of course, the first thing we receive in prayer is a calm spirit, and we shed the need to plunge into a panicky flood of words.

This is why this pattern of prayer begins with a word of relationship: *Father.* It is essential to know to whom we are praying. When we come to God in prayer, we are not talking *about* God, nor are we engaging in a theological dialogue. We are experiencing fellowship *with* God. We are talking to God the Father and listening to God the Father. And since we converse directly with Him, it is essential that we understand to whom we are speaking. Our Lord gathers it all up in this marvelously expressive word *Father* and says true prayer must begin with a concept of our relationship to God as our loving but holy heavenly Father.

Immediately, this sense of our relationship to Him as our Father eliminates a number of false conceptions regarding God. It shows us that prayer, real prayer, is never to be addressed to the Chairman of the Committee for Welfare and Relief. Sometimes our prayers take on that tone. We come expecting a handout. We want something to be poured into our laps, something we think we need. In making an appeal to Him, we are only filling out the properly prescribed forms. That's not authentic prayer.

Nor is prayer addressed to the Chief of the Bureau of Investigation. Prayer is never to be merely a confession of our wrongdoings, with the hope that we may cast ourselves upon the mercy of the court.

Nor is it an appeal to the Secretary of the Treasury, some sort of genial international banker whom we hope to interest in financing our projects.

No, authentic prayer is an intimate conversation with the Father—the God who possesses a father's heart, a father's love, a father's strength, and a father's concern for the best interests of His children. The first and truest note of prayer must be our recognition that we come to this kind of father. We must hear Him and come to Him as a child, in trust and simplicity and with all the frankness of a child—otherwise it is not prayer.

The word *father* answers all the philosophical questions about the nature of God. A father is a person; therefore, God is not a blind force behind the inscrutable machinery of the universe. A father is able to hear; therefore, God is not some impersonal being, aloof from all our troubles and problems. And above all, a father is predisposed by love and relationship to give a careful, attentive ear to what his child says. God is like that. From a father a child can surely expect a reply. And when we pray, we are talking to our Father.

Our Lord goes on to teach us more of what a father is like in the parable that follows this prayer:

> "Which of you fathers, if your son asks for a fish,
> will give him a snake instead? Or if he asks for an egg,
> will give him a scorpion? If you then, though you are

evil, know how to give good gifts to your children, how much more will your Father in heaven give the Holy Spirit to those who ask him!" (Luke 11:11–13).

The point is that God, being a loving Father, is interested in what we have to say. A father can be expected to respond to our pleas.

We are not only to address God as "Father"—that is, by simply saying the word with our lips. We are to *believe* that He is a Father, and relate to Him as a Father, for all that God makes available to us must always come to us through faith, must always operate in our lives through a trusting belief in Him. Belief invariably involves not just an intellectual agreement with a set of creeds, but an actual commitment of the will, a moving of the deepest part of our heart. Belief is not expressed by addressing God as "Almighty God" or "Dreadful Creator" or "Ground of all Being." Such grandiose terms actually betray our fatal ignorance or unbelief! The greatest authority on prayer says that God is a *loving, caring, providing Father!*

When I come home, I do not want my children to meet me in awe and terror, chanting, "Oh, thou great and dreadful Pastor of Peninsula Bible Church, welcome to this unworthy and miserable home." It would be an insult to my father-heart. I want my children to greet me as a father. It is never prayer until we recognize that we are coming to a patient and tender father. That is the first note in true prayer.

Dark Closets

The second note of true prayer is one of surrender: "Hallowed be your name." I am sure this is the petition that makes hypocrites out of most of us. We may be able to say "Father" with grateful sincerity, but when we pray, "Hallowed be your name," we say this with the guilty knowledge that there are areas of our lives in which His name is not hallowed, and in which we truly don't want it to be hallowed.

Hallowed means holy and honored. When we say, "Hallowed be your name," we are praying, "May the whole of my life be a source of delight to you and may it be an honor to the name which I bear, which is your name." We find the same sense in this prayer of David's from the psalms: "May the words of my mouth and the meditation of my heart be pleasing in your sight, O LORD, my Rock and my Redeemer" (Psalm 19:14).

The trouble is that we have great areas of our lives that are not hallowed. We have reserved to ourselves certain monopolies, privileged areas that we do not wish to surrender, where the name of our career ambition or the name of some person or the name of our sinful habit or the name of the almighty dollar is more dear and hallowed to us than the name of God.

But when we pray, "Hallowed be your name," if there is any degree whatsoever of sincerity or honesty, we are really praying, "Lord, I open to you every closet; I am taking every skeleton out for you to examine. Hallowed be your name in every compartment of my life." We cannot have any contact with God, any real touch of His power, any genuine experience of the glorious fragrance and wonder of God at work in our lives until we truly pray, "Hallowed be your name in my life."

Notice that this prayer is not phrased simply as a confession or an expression of repentance to the Father. We are not to pray as we so frequently do, "Father, help me to be good," or "Help me to be better." Isn't it rather remarkable that throughout this whole pattern prayer not once is a desire for help in the sanctification of life expressed? Many of our primary concerns and so many concerns of Scripture are never reflected in this prayer.

Instead, Jesus turns our attention entirely away from ourselves and toward the Father. This phrase, "Hallowed be your name," is really a cry of helpless trust, in which we are simply standing and saying, "Father, not only do I know that there are areas in my life where your name is not hallowed, but I know also that only you can hallow them. I am quite willing to simply stand still and let you be the Holy One who will actually be first in my life."

When we pray according to Jesus' instruction, sanctification naturally follows. Whenever we let God be our Lord and surrender everything to Him we are drawn quite spontaneously into a great learning process. We can't help becoming different people. Martin Luther once said, "You do not command a stone which is lying in the sun to be warm. It will be warm all by itself."

We are truly saying, "Hallowed be your name," whenever we say, "Father, there is no area of my life that I hide from you. Search me, illuminate the dark corners of my life. Reveal to me the flaws and sin in my relationships, my social life, my sex life, my thought life, my business life, my school life, my recreation and vacation times." When we pray that way, we discover that God will walk into the dark closets of our life—places where the stench of our sin is so great we cannot even bear it—and He will clean them out and make them fit for His dwelling. "If we walk in the light," John tells us, "as he is in the light, we have fellowship with one another, and the blood of Jesus, his Son, purifies us from all sin" (1 John 1:7).

To walk in the light does not mean to live sinlessly—that is impossible while we are in these bodies, living in this world. It means living honestly and openly before God, so that the light of His truth can illuminate and cleanse the dark corners of our lives.

Kingdom Hope

The third cry of true prayer also begins with God—and it is a cry of hope: "Your kingdom come." Now, this can be a sigh for heaven. Who does not feel homesick for heaven, longing to be free from the humdrum sameness of life, and experiencing the glory we read of in the Bible?

Or this can be, as it ought to be, a cry for heaven to come to earth. In other words, "May the kingdoms of this world become the kingdom of our Lord and of His Christ." This is the expectation expressed in the words of the old hymn,

> Jesus shall reign where'er the sun
> Does his successive journeys run;
> His kingdom stretch from shore to shore,
> Till moons shall wax and wane no more.

Scripture often mentions this, and all of us long for that day to come when God will rule in righteousness over all the earth.

But I think this prayer means more than that. It is more than a long, wistful look into the future, whether on earth or off the earth. It is a cry that God's will may be done right now, in the midst of the blood and sweat and tears of life. In other words, "Your kingdom come through what I am going through at this very moment." This is our kingdom hope—a hope not only for a future in heaven but a hope that our present trials can be used as part of God's plan.

Scripture reveals to us a truth that we never could know by ourselves, but which becomes self-evident as we look at life through the lens of God's Word. That is, God, in a manner of speaking, builds His kingdom in secret. God is often accomplishing the most when it is least evident that He is at work. Behind the scaffolding of tragedy and despair, God frequently builds His empire of love and glory. When we think God is silent, when we feel God has removed His hand and we no longer sense the warmth of His presence, God frequently is at work accomplishing the greatest good for ourselves, for others, and for His eternal plan.

God's Building Materials

I once talked with a young man who had gone through a fearsome accident that had left a disfiguring mark on him. Yet that physical scar was nothing compared with the scarring pain he experienced when his marriage dissolved. He had been raised in the church, and had once looked on those who went through pain and problems with a self-righteous disdain. But, he told me, "The humiliation of my divorce cut the ground right out from under my self-righteous attitude. I know I never would have learned to feel for others and experience the joy of God's purpose for my life if I had not become a divorce statistic." These are the ways that God builds His kingdom. What a mystery this is! As the poet wrote,

> God moves in a mysterious way
> His wonders to perform;
> He plants His footsteps in the sea,
> And rides upon the storm.
>
> Ye fearful saints, fresh courage take;
> The clouds ye so much dread

Are filled with mercies, and shall break
In blessings 'round thy head.

Can any liturgy or ritual of the church speak this more eloquently to us than the Lord's Supper? When we gather for the breaking of bread and the drinking of wine, we remember that each is a symbol of the pain, anguish, and sorrow of the bitter death our Lord went through. But, as Cowper writes,

Deep in unfathomable mines
Of never-failing skill
He treasures up His bright designs,
And works His sovereign will.

Out of darkness God calls forth light; out of despair, hope. From death comes resurrection. You cannot have resurrection without death, hope without despair, or light without darkness. By means of defeat the kingdom of God is born in human hearts.

This is the meaning of prayer: "Oh, Lord, I am but a little child. I do not understand the mysteries of life. I do not know your ways in this world, but Lord, I pray that through these circumstances in which I now find myself—these painful troubles and struggles—your kingdom come." The transforming agent is prayer—simple, trusting prayer, rising out of the helpless need of a child to touch a father's heart.

Father, how frequently we misunderstand life even though you have gone to such great lengths to show us the secret of life. How many times, Father, have we rebelled foolishly against you and your workings in our lives? How many times have we turned away from you? And yet, have

we not also seen that through these hours of resentment and burning shame and bitterness, you have been lovingly at work to teach us the truth and to bring us to an understanding of reality, to bring us back to your loving heart? Father, hallowed be your name. Your kingdom come—both in the world to come and in the world we live in every day.

In Jesus' name, Amen.

5

When Prayer Becomes Personal

"Give us each day our daily bread. Forgive us our sins, for we also forgive everyone who sins against us. And lead us not into temptation."

Luke 11:3–4

The Lord's Prayer consists of exactly 66 words in the King James Version. The Gettysburg Address is made up of 286 words. The Declaration of Independence is comprised of 1,322 words. However, federal regulations governing the sale of a head of cabbage total 26,911 words. These statistics suggest a fascinating principle: The wiser, grander, and more profound the idea to be expressed, the fewer words are needed to express it. In the Lord's Prayer we find that Jesus has reduced to the simplest and most elegant terms some of the most mighty and life-changing themes of our existence. If we could grasp the grand truths of life that He has captured for us in these few words, our lives and relationships would be utterly transformed!

In the previous chapter, we examined the first part of this magnificent model prayer—the part that relates to God the Father, His glory and holiness, His kingdom in heaven and on earth, and our need to submit to His will. Now we come to the part of the prayer that deals directly with our own experience of life, our behavior, our relationships, our moral character. This is a prayer for the whole human being—body, soul, and spirit. With pinpoint accuracy, Jesus targets each of these areas of our lives, so that if we understand this prayer properly, and pray it as it should be prayed, nothing further really needs to be said.

I believe one of the great tragedies surrounding the Lord's Prayer is that we have turned it into a religious ritual, and so we have missed its profound and practical meaning for our lives. This prayer was never intended to be merely repeated over and over in some mechanical fashion, like a Buddhist chant. Our Lord gave it to us as a guide to a vital, practical prayer life. Each of these short phrases is infinitely expandable as to detail—and Jesus fully expects each of us to fill in the details! We are to pray this prayer in our hearts, specifically listing the sins we have committed, then specifically listing the people who have offended us, asking God for strength to forgive them every time that twinge of anger or bitterness arises in us!

If we as Christians will use this prayer as a model for authentic interaction with God, and not as a meaningless Christian mantra, then our lives will be changed and our churches will be transformed—guaranteed!

Praying for the Body

Jesus begins this section of the prayer with the needs of the body. I like that! We have such a distorted concept of prayer that we often feel that we shouldn't pray about physical needs. That is a reflection of a pagan—not Christian!—concept of life. The Greeks regarded the body as coarse and unworthy of redemption, and they therefore mistreated it. They tortured and tormented their bodies. This idea that the body must be either neglected or subdued by physical mistreatment is widespread in Asian cultures today, but you never find this in New Testament Christianity.

Some might point to Philippians 3:21, which speaks of Jesus Christ "who, by the power that enables him to bring everything under his control, will transform our lowly bodies so that they will be like his glorious body." Some translations use the word *vile* instead of *lowly*, meaning that the body is somehow repulsive and disgusting. But that's not what the original Greek word means. This verse describes the body as being lowly in the sense that it is not yet glorified. It has not yet entered into the ultimate state for which God has designed it. But Paul is not saying that there is anything wrong with the body.

God likes bodies. That may startle you, but it is true that God engineered and designed them, and He likes them. He cares about our health and physical well-being, and it is perfectly proper for us to pray about the needs of the body. Bread, as expressed in the prayer, is a symbol of all the necessities of physical life; it stands for all that our physical life demands—shelter, water, food, exercise, clothing—anything the body requires.

The vital concern expressed here is that an immediate and sufficient supply be made available to us. The only limit in this prayer is that we are never to pray for a warehouse, a full supply for a year ahead. Each day we are to pray for *that day's* supply.

The question this prayer poses to you and me is this: Do we pray daily for our physical needs? Do we take time to ask God for them, or at least give thanks for them? Perhaps this has become such a familiar request in the repeating of the Lord's Prayer that it has lost any real meaning for us and we do not take it seriously. This may be the most flagrant and frequent area of Christian disobedience. After all, our Lord meant it when He told us to pray, "give us each day our daily bread."

I am sure that the Lord must have had some good reason for telling us to pray in this particular way. Some will argue that Jesus said elsewhere, "Your Father knows what you need before you ask him" (Matthew 6:8), so the purpose of this prayer is not to inform God of our needs. Others say it really makes little difference whether or not we pray about physical things because we receive the necessities of life, regardless. So, what's the point of praying?

Obviously, prayer is not a means by which we inform God of our needs. Prayer is not so much a channel by which we influence God as it is a channel through which God influences us! It is we who need prayer, not Him. He already knows our needs, because He knows everything about us. But prayer is something we need.

Just ask yourself what happens when you neglect to pray for your daily needs and to thank God for His daily provision of blessings. If you honestly examine your life over an extended period of prayerlessness, you will see that a slow, subtle, but inevitable change steals over your heart. You begin to take His blessings for granted and gradually succumb to the foolish delusion that you have provided all those blessings yourself! That is the path to vanity. Prayer is the path to wisdom—the active, grateful realization that all we have and all we are and all we are able to accomplish comes directly from Him. Prayerlessness leads to pride and blindness—a blindness that darkens our spiritual insight, making us cynical, anxious, restless, and depressed. Prayer leads to humility and spiritual wholeness.

Human—or Dog?

The book of Daniel describes the spiritual pride of Nebuchadnezzar, proud king of Babylon. In the evening, he walked out on the battlements of his palace, looked out over the city, and said, "Is not this the great Babylon I have built as the royal residence, by my mighty power and for the glory of my majesty?" (Daniel 4:30). He reveled in what he thought were his own powers, which he credited for the splendor he saw.

As a result of that defiant assumption about the basic powers of supply in his life, God brought upon him the judgment of bestiality. He became a beast, and was turned out to eat grass in the fields like an animal. This was God's dramatic way of saying that ingratitude causes people to become animal-like, with all the mindless ferocity and self-centeredness of beasts growling over their food.

Dr. H. A. Ironside once told of an occasion when, as a young man, he went into a cafeteria to eat. He took his tray and looked for a place to sit, but found all the seats occupied except one chair opposite a man seated at a table. So Dr. Ironside approached the man and asked if he might sit down. The man looked up, nodded his head, and grunted something unintelligible. Dr. Ironside sat down and, as was his custom, bowed his head and silently gave thanks for his food. When he looked up, he saw the man glowering at him. "What's the matter?" the fellow asked gruffly. "Something wrong with your food?"

"No," Dr. Ironside responded, "it seems all right to me."

The man persisted: "Have you got a headache, or something?"

"No," Ironside answered, "I feel fine. Why do you ask?"

"Well, I noticed you bowing down and putting your hand up to your head and closing your eyes. I thought maybe there was something wrong with your head."

"No," Dr. Ironside replied, "I was simply returning thanks to God for my food."

The man snorted derisively and said, "Oh, you believe in that bosh, do you?"

"Don't you ever give thanks?"

"Nah," the man sneered. "I don't believe in giving thanks for anything. I just start right in."

"Ah," said Dr. Ironside cheerfully, "you're just like my dog!"

"Huh?" The man looked puzzled—and annoyed.

"My dog never gives thanks, either," Dr. Ironside explained. "He just starts right in!" And the other man had nothing more to say.

The fact is, God doesn't need our prayers and our thanks—but we certainly need to give thanks to God! If we fail to remind ourselves whose hand has provided all we have, then we become like Dr. Ironside's dog—brutishly digging in to life's blessings, never elevating our spirit to recognize and commune with the One who provided those blessings in the first place.

Everything we have comes from God's hand, and it could all be stripped from us in a moment. Our daily bread, and even our moment-to-moment respiration and heartbeat, come to us purely by His grace and His goodness. To avoid the brutish sin of ingratitude, we must follow the example of Christ, praying daily to the Father, constantly remembering that

> Back of the bread is the snowy flour
> And back of the flour, the mill
> And back of the mill is the field of wheat,
> The rain, and the Father's will.

A Prayer for Relationships

Junior had been trying his mother's patience all day. Finally, Mom had had enough and sent Junior to his room. Later, after he had served his sentence, Junior was allowed out of his room on parole. "Mom," he said, "I prayed about our problem while I was in my room."

Mom was delighted to hear it. "That's wonderful, Junior," she said. "If you ask God to help you be good, He will help you."

"Oh, I didn't ask God to help me be good," replied Junior. "I asked Him to help you put up with me."

Well, this little boy didn't quite grasp the "lead us not into temptation" part of prayer—but he did understand that prayer is a crucial factor in healing strained relationships!

For that, in fact, is the focus of the second request of the Lord's Prayer. In this passage, the model prayer of Jesus moves into the area of human relationships, our conscious life, emotions, intellect, and will. This is the section that deals with the human soul.

Here our Lord touches on the central issue in this area of life: forgiveness. "Forgive us our sins," Jesus teaches, "for we also forgive everyone who sins against us." This prayer addresses the need for a cleansed conscience, for a sense of peace, for reconciliation of ourselves with God and with one another. God knew that the emotional clutter of our life takes a very deadly toll on us, so He created this path of cleansing through prayer.

Who of us has never experienced the painful results of imagined illnesses? Not that they are really imaginary, for they are actually the physical symptoms that arise from disarray in our emotional life. Familiar to all of us are such symptoms as palpitations of the heart, shortness of breath, skin rashes, throbbing migraine headaches that seem to split the skull, stammering, stuttering, nervous compulsions, and more. Then there are the really troublesome mental symptoms: morbid depression, anxiety, irrational apprehension, bitterness, insecurity, and so on.

Where do all these grinning physical and emotional demons come from? Both Scripture and modern psychology agree that underneath these symptoms lurk two frightening monsters: fear and guilt. If only we could slay these fiery dragons, the whole emotional atmosphere of our lives would finally be at peace.

In this simple prayer that Jesus gives us we find a mighty sword for dragon-slaying. When we pray, "Forgive us our sins," we are asking for the reality that God promises to every believer in Jesus Christ, "There is now no condemnation for those who are in Christ Jesus" (Romans 8:1). I don't know of anything that troubles Christians more than a sense of guilt, of self-condemnation. Guilt is the most frequent problem behind the distressing ailments evident in many a Christian's experience, but in this simple prayer we find a fully adequate answer. For if we have laid hold of the forgiveness of God, we know that nothing lies between us and the Lord. Our hearts are absolutely free before Him and the result is a pervading sense of peace.

But Jesus immediately adds a limitation: We cannot ask God to forgive our sins unless we are willing to forgive those who sin against us.

I want to head off any confusion at this point. Jesus is certainly not referring here to the divine forgiveness that accompanies conversion. The Lord's Prayer is meant for Christians, because only Christians can really pray it intelligently. No non-Christian ever receives forgiveness from God on the basis of claiming to forgive anyone else. No one can authentically forgive in a Christlike way who has not received the forgiveness of God. That forgiveness is offered on the basis of Jesus' death.

Paul says, "In him we have redemption through his blood, the forgiveness of sins, in accordance with the riches of God's grace" (Ephesians 1:7). God's grace—that's all! We come thanking Him for what Jesus' death on the cross has already done in taking away the awful burden of our sin. But, though we have received that forgiveness, we will never be able to enjoy forgiveness from the defilements of our Christian walk unless we are ready to extend it freely to those who offend us. Such forgiveness keeps us enjoying unbroken fellowship with the Father and with the Son, which is, of course, the secret of emotional quietness and rest.

As a Christian it is useless to pray, "Father, forgive my sins," if you hold a grudge against someone else, or burn with resentment and bitterness. Our instructions are clear: "First go and be reconciled to your brother; then come and offer your gift" (Matthew 5:24). Forgive your brother, and then the healing forgiveness of God will flood your own heart. You will find then that nothing can destroy the God-given peace down at the very center of your being. If we refuse to forgive someone else, we are really withholding from another the grace that has already been shown to us. It is only because we have already been forgiven the great and staggering debt of our own sins that we can ever find the grace to forgive the relatively insignificant slights others have put upon us.

A man once said to me, "I know I'm a Christian, but someone once did an awful thing to me—something I just can't forget or forgive."

I replied, "Are you sure that you can't forgive him?"

He maintained that he had really tried to forgive this man, but was unable to do so. As we continued talking, I said, "You know, I have found that we often use the word *can't* when what we really mean is *won't*. Isn't it possible that what you are saying is not, 'I *can't* forgive him,' but 'I *won't* forgive him'? If it is really true that you cannot forgive this man, then it indicates that you yourself have never been forgiven and you are only kidding yourself about being a Christian."

This shook him a bit. He thought it through and then, with rather a sheepish grin, he said, "I guess you're right. I guess it is *won't*." It wasn't long before he came back to me and reported with joy that he had finally forgiven the man who had injured him.

If we take these words seriously, what a revolution this will make in our lives, in our homes, and in our churches! We will never discover what God means in terms of the sweetness of forgiving grace in our own lives and hearts if we are not willing to melt the black frost of bitter years of withered, broken relationships.

Dealing With Temptation

The third area of prayer is in the realm of the spirit: "And lead us not into temptation." Again, Jesus penetrates to the vital core of the matter. In the unseen war of the spirit, the greatest needs of our lives are deliverance and protection. But an immediate problem arises here, for Scripture reveals that temptation is necessary to us and no Christian escapes it. Furthermore, though God Himself never tempts us to sin, He does test us with difficult and discouraging circumstances, and these become the instruments of God to strengthen us, to build us up, and to give us victory.

When we read this portion of the Lord's Prayer, we are confronted with this question: Are we really expected to pray that God will not do what He must do to accomplish His work within us? After all, even Jesus, we are told, was led by the Spirit into the wilderness to be tempted by the devil.

So what does He mean, then, when He says, "And lead us not into temptation"? I have puzzled and prayed and read about this issue over the years. I am now convinced that what Jesus meant is that we should pray to be kept from unrecognized temptation. When temptation is recognized, it can be resisted, and when we resist, it is always a source of strength and growth in our lives. If I am filling out my income tax and find that some income has come to me through other than ordinary channels and there is no way of anyone checking it, I am confronted with a temptation to omit it. But I know that is wrong. No one has to tell me; I know it. And when I resist that, I find I am stronger the next time when an even larger amount may be involved.

You see, it is a rather simple matter to resist obvious evil, if we really mean to walk with God. But temptation is not always so easily discerned. There are times when I feel sure I am right, and with utmost sincerity and integrity of heart I do what I believe is the right thing, but later I look back and see that I was horribly wrong. I believe that is what Jesus is talking about in this part of the prayer.

Peter is an example of this. In the Upper Room, with brash confidence and utter naiveté, Peter said to the Lord,

"Even if all fall away on account of you, I never will."

"I tell you the truth," Jesus answered, "this very night, before the rooster crows, you will disown me three times."

But Peter declared, "Even if I have to die with you, I will never disown you." And all the other disciples said the same (Matthew 26:33–35).

Still confident, Peter went into the Garden of Gethsemane and when the soldiers came, he cut off the ear of the high priest's servant in his eagerness to show his faithfulness to the Lord. Earlier Jesus had said to him in the garden, "Watch and pray so that you will not fall into temptation. The spirit is willing, but the body is weak" (Matthew 26:41). But Peter didn't heed that word. Instead he slept, and after waking him our Lord again asked him to pray—not for the Lord, but for himself.

But Peter did not pray, and when he came into the court of the high priest and was standing before the fire, Satan wrung out his courage and hung him up to dry. There, with cursing and swearing, Peter found himself trapped. He denied his Lord, and in the awful realization of what he had done, Peter went out into the blackness of the night and wept bitterly. This is what our Lord refers to in the phrase, "Lead us not into temptation." This prayer is the recognition of our foolish weakness and our tendency to stumble into blind folly.

Living in Dependence on God

When Hudson Taylor, that intrepid missionary to China, was only a young man, he journeyed from Swatow up to the great city of Shanghai, earnestly seeking to do God's will. There he planned to get his medical instruments and medicines and return with them to the city of Swatow where he expected to labor with a Scottish missionary who had formerly been his companion there. Arriving in Shanghai, he discovered that the building in which he had left all his supplies and instruments had burned to the ground. All was lost.

Baffled and discouraged, unable to fathom why God would allow such a disaster, he sat down and pondered. Then, with hardly any money in his pockets, he got up and made his way along the network of canals to the city of Ningpo where he could buy some supplies from another missionary, then take a boat back to Swatow. In the heat of summer, he journeyed, preaching as he went.

Arriving at the end of the canals, Hudson Taylor hired some local Chinese workers to carry his baggage. He started out and soon outdistanced the Chinese baggage carriers, and finally had to wait through one long, hot afternoon for them to catch up. To his dismay he discovered when they finally arrived that they were all opium-smokers and would be unable to carry the load over the distance ahead. So he dismissed most of them, retaining only the leader of the group, whom he delegated to hire more baggage carriers. Then he started out once more. Soon he had to stop again—and this time the baggage carriers did not catch up. In fact, he never saw them or his baggage again.

Completely discouraged, he went to an inn for a night's sleep and found it rat-infested and bug-ridden. He hardly slept. The next morning he pressed on to the coast and, after a long, hot, discouraging march, he entered a city to find someplace to sleep. He was turned away by several inns because he was a foreigner. Then the police began to shadow him, and he didn't know where to turn.

Finally, a young man offered to help him. Together they trudged around the city without success until one o'clock in the morning, and then the young man abandoned him. He had to spend the rest of the night on the steps of a temple with three thieves lurking in the shadows, waiting for him to fall asleep so they could murder him and take his few possessions. Taylor stayed awake the rest of the night, singing hymns and repeating Bible verses to himself until the thieves gave up in disgust and left. Only then did he manage to catch a few moments' sleep.

In the morning the young man who had taken him through the city streets came back and demanded an outrageous fee for his "guide service." This was too much. Hudson Taylor lost his temper, grabbed the fellow by the arm, shook him, and told him to go away. Weary, broken, and dispirited, he started the long, painful journey back to Shanghai. For eight long miles he dragged himself along in spiritual rebellion, wondering why God had abandoned him.

Then it came to him: He had denied his Lord, just as Peter had! All his anger and pain melted into tears of repentance as the truth broke through to him that he had never asked God's guidance and protection along the way. He had been so intent upon his own trouble that he had forgotten to commit the matter to the Lord.

He wrote in his journal that, as he went along, he confessed his prayerlessness and faithlessness to God, asking the Lord to forgive him. And at that moment his heart was flooded with a glorious sense of the presence and forgiveness of Christ. The initiative and control passed once again from Hudson Taylor to the Lord where it belonged.

This was what God wanted. When Taylor got to Shanghai, he found a letter waiting for him with a check in it for the exact amount needed to cover his losses. And he learned soon afterward that if he had gone on to Swatow, he would have arrived just in time to be imprisoned, and perhaps executed. All the worry, fear, despair, and perplexity he experienced was totally unnecessary. The events might have been the same, regardless of whether he prayed or not, but the emotions he experienced would have been far different if only he had prayed, "Lord, lead me not into temptation."

All three of the requests in the Lord's Prayer reflect the one great truth that Jesus labors to impress upon us: We are forever in need—body, soul, and spirit. Only as we walk in continual, step-by-step dependence upon the living God can any of these needs be adequately met. When we fail to pray, we fail to depend on Him. We condemn ourselves to physical, emotional, and spiritual starvation. But when we pray continually, maintaining our heartfelt connection with God through an authentic prayer life modeled on this simple, childlike prayer, we guard our souls against upset and failure. We bind our hearts to the heart of the One who created the universe, the One who loved us enough to send His Son to us.

Jesus died for us. He rose for us. He taught us how to pray. He showed us how to live in dependence on the Father. He is our example, and our part is simply to imitate Him.

Our Father, we can only echo these words our Lord Jesus taught us. Give us this day our daily bread, forgive us our sins, lead us not into temptation.

In Christ's name, Amen.

Part Two

Asking, seeking, or knocking—the answer is certain, if we believe God. Faith takes His answer for granted.

The fulfillment of all our need is an activity of the Holy Spirit—and yet, mysteriously, He waits until we ask before He moves! The invisible events of heaven, which will be reflected on earth, are determined in the heart of a praying Christian. Because Jesus went to the Father, He has promised to do through us works of lasting, eternal value—even *greater* works, in fact, than the works He did while on earth!

A Christian's work is never anything but borrowed activity, based on borrowed authority—authority borrowed from God.

6

Prayer's Certainties

He said to them, "Suppose one of you has a friend,
and he goes to him at midnight and says, 'Friend, lend me
three loaves of bread, because a friend of mine on a jour-
ney has come to me, and I have nothing to set before him.'

"Then the one inside answers, 'Don't bother me. The
door is already locked, and my children are with me in
bed. I can't get up and give you anything.' I tell you,
though he will not get up and give him the bread because
he is his friend, yet because of the man's boldness he will
get up and give him as much as he needs.

"So I say to you: Ask and it will be given to you; seek
and you will find; knock and the door will be opened to
you. For everyone who asks receives; he who seeks finds;
and to him who knocks, the door will be opened.

"Which of you fathers, if your son asks for a fish, will
give him a snake instead? Or if he asks for an egg, will give
him a scorpion? If you then, though you are evil, know
how to give good gifts to your children, how much more
will your Father in heaven give the Holy Spirit to those
who ask him!"

Luke 11:5–13

"Lord, teach us to pray," begged the disciple.

As we have seen in the preceding chapters, the Lord responded to that plea and taught His disciples a model prayer, which He intended us to use as a guide. Immediately after giving us this model prayer, which has come to be called the Lord's Prayer, Jesus expands on His response to the disciple's plea by telling a story—the familiar parable of the obstinate friend in Luke 11:5–13. The lesson Jesus wants us to learn from this parable is found in the introduction:

> He said to them, "Suppose one of you has a friend, and he goes to him at midnight and says, 'Friend, lend me three loaves of bread, because a friend of mine on a journey has come to me, and I have nothing to set before him.'
>
> "Then the one inside answers, 'Don't bother me. The door is already locked, and my children are with me in bed. I can't get up and give you anything' " (Luke 11:5–7).

The link with prayer in this story is obvious: *True prayer never occurs apart from a sense of need.* The first note in the story Jesus tells is one of dire, pressing necessity. Here a man comes to a friend after midnight and announces that he has unexpected company arriving after a long journey—he has nothing in the house to serve his company, and he demands that the friend help him out.

The needs of others often seem more urgent and pressing to us than our own needs. I doubt that this man would ever have gone to his friend's house in the middle of the night to borrow bread to meet his own hunger. But when company arrives after a long journey, a deep sense of necessity makes him willing to go to his neighbor to ask for bread even though it is late and he knows his neighbor is in bed.

There is a note of audacity here. Not many of us today would even think of troubling a friend after midnight for a mere loaf of bread! As someone has said, "He may not have any bread, but he certainly has plenty of crust!" Yet it is obvious, as our Lord tells the story (and he tells it with a touch of humor that I'm sure was intentional), that this man is driven by a deep sense of concern. He simply has nothing to give his hungry friend and is forced to go to his neighbor for help. Is anything quite so likely to bring us to our knees in prayer as the request of another person for our help, and the shattering awareness that we simply have nothing to give?

What Shall I Say?

One evening around ten o'clock, my telephone rang. I picked it up and recognized the voice of a young man, a relatively new Christian who had been steadily maturing in his newfound faith. That night, however, he was very troubled and there was a note of desperation in his voice. "My wife just phoned me," he said. "She's out someplace with a girl-friend of hers, and she wants to bring this woman home to talk to me."

"Why is that?"

"Well, my wife's girlfriend is a good friend from their college days together. This woman is an unmarried schoolteacher and she's been going through some very tough times lately. Fact is, she told my wife she is contemplating suicide."

"And your wife thinks you can help this woman by talking to her?" I asked.

"That's right," the young man replied. "She says that, since I'm a Christian, I should be able to say something to this young woman that will help her with her problems, so she won't be suicidal anymore."

"Why does your wife think you can help, just because you are a Christian?" I asked. "Your wife is not a Christian, is she?"

"No, she's not. In fact, she's been very resistant to the gospel and has really been harassing me because of my faith."

"But now that her friend is suicidal, she thinks the Christian faith may have something to offer."

"That's right," said the young man. "But Pastor Stedman, I'm in a panic! I mean, what can I say? What if I say the wrong thing? I'm just a new Christian—not a pastor or a counselor! What should I say to her?"

Perhaps you know how my young friend felt. You may know that strange, sinking sensation when someone asks for help and you do not know what to say. Immediately you have a sense of pressure, responsibility, or even terror. "What shall I say?" Perhaps a neighbor comes for coffee and suddenly a question arises or a problem is laid bare. Or a school friend stammers out a question as you are walking to class together. Or a letter arrives from a friend or relative with an urgent plea. Or a friend invites you out to lunch, then tells you he or she is contemplating divorce or having an affair or diagnosed with an incurable disease or dealing with some other loss, tragedy, sin, or difficult decision. And you only have time for one brief, panicky prayer, "Lord, what shall I say?"

It is as if you are rushing to your great neighbor, God, after midnight, knocking on His door out of your great sense of need and inadequacy. It is as if you are crying out to Him, "Lord, I need to give this person bread and I have nothing to give! Please give me bread to share with this person!" It is out of such moments of deep necessity that true prayer is born.

In this parable, our Lord immediately moves on to sound a note of absolute certainty:

> "I say to you: Ask and it will be given to you; seek and you will find; knock and the door will be opened to you. For everyone who asks receives; he who seeks finds; and to him who knocks, the door will be opened" (Luke 11:9–10).

What an amazing declaration! The implications are staggering. Some interpret verse 8 as though our Lord is saying that we must wear God down with our prayers. They suggest that the only way we can expect to get anything from God is to be relentless and obstinate in prayer, to hound God until He tires, gives in, and answers our request.

I am absolutely convinced, however, that Jesus is teaching precisely the *opposite!* Note that in the parables of the importunate widow and the ungodly judge (see chapter 1), as well as in this parable of the obstinate friend, Jesus sets before us a stark contrast to illuminate the truth He wants us to learn. In fact, He goes on to say—clearly and unmistakably—that God is not like that sleepy, reluctant neighbor who doesn't want to get up out of bed. With God, He says, "Everyone who asks receives; he who seeks finds; and to him who knocks, the door will be opened," and He compares God to a caring father who eagerly, lovingly gives good gifts.

Sometimes, when our prayers seem to fail, we blame ourselves for not being persistent enough. We find prayer irksome, difficult, and unpleasant, and we say, "I know I should pray more; I know if I did, greater things would happen." We are obsessed with the completely unbiblical idea that God is a reluctant God who must be wheedled and badgered into blessing us.

But, says Jesus, that is not what God the Father is like. God gives willingly, freely, without fail, to every child who comes to Him. Even earthly fathers do not give capriciously, vindictively, or cruelly—much less would your loving Father in heaven.

Ask, Seek, Knock

Note carefully what Jesus goes on to say about prayer, for He suggests that there are three levels of prayer: ask, seek, and knock. (You can remember them, incidentally, if you will notice that the initial letters of each word spell "ask," *a* for ask, *s* for seek, and *k* for knock.) The circumstances of each of these three levels of prayer are vastly different, yet the answer is always the same.

Level 1: Ask. The simplest and easiest level, of course, is simply to ask. What Jesus means is that certain needs require a mere asking to be immediately and invariably met, and the range of these needs is far wider than we usually give God credit for. For instance, in reading through the New Testament, it becomes clear that our need for Christlike attributes lies in this category. If we need love, courage, wisdom, power, patience, we are to simply ask, that is all. Ask, and the answer is immediately given.

Isn't that what James says? "If any of you lacks wisdom, *he should ask God*, who gives generously to all without finding fault, and it will be given to him" (James 1:5, emphasis added). That's all; ask, and it shall be given.

But, we protest, "I have tried this. Not long ago I was in a situation in which I felt I didn't know the answer, so I sent up a prayer, 'Lord, help me, give me wisdom'—and nothing happened! I went into that situation and did the most inane and foolish things! Prayer just doesn't work."

What are we saying? Is God a liar? Does He say He will give and then fail to do so? Is He like a cruel, wicked father who gives us a scorpion when we ask for an egg, or a snake when we ask for a fish? No, the question is not, "Did God give?" but, "Did I receive? Did I ask in faith? Did I believe God when I asked? Did I take the answer He gave?" Remember that James goes on to say:

> But when he asks, he must believe and not doubt, because he who doubts is like a wave of the sea, blown and tossed by the wind. That man should not think he will receive anything from the Lord; he is a double-minded man, unstable in all he does (James 1:6–8).

All God's gifts are given to faith, not to unbelief. The problem here is: What do you do after you have asked? What were you expecting when you asked God for wisdom? How did you think He would give it? Were you waiting for a sense of wisdom, some kind of clarifying of the brain or increased mental power so that you could see all the answers clearly? Were you expecting a feeling of power, some tingling electric charge to run down your backbone and out to the end of your nerves? Is this what you were waiting for?

No, faith takes the answer for granted. God is faithful. We know that God gives to those who ask. When we ask, we must take it for granted that He has given. Then, whatever word comes to our lips, we must count on the fact that it is the very word of wisdom or the word of courage or the word of patience that we need. God loves to be trusted, but only faith can lay hold of what He gives. When faith is there, the need is invariably met.

When Jesus says, "Ask, and it shall be given," He does not say the answer will be accompanied by any feelings, signs, or emotions. Just take it for granted, thank God for His answer, step out in faith on His answer, and the answer will certainly be there.

Level 2: Seek. A second level of prayer is denoted by the word *seek.* You cannot think of what it means to seek without understanding that the word in the original language suggests an element of time. Seeking is not a single act. It is a process, a series of acts.

Every mother knows that husbands and children think of seeking as a single act. When looking for a lost object, they will stand in the middle of a room, cast one sweeping glance around, then call for help: "Mom, where is so-and-so?" And mother opens the drawers, moves the bottle, lifts the stack of magazines—and there it is. I'm convinced my wife is a master of sleight-of-hand, for I cannot understand how, when she looks for it, an object will suddenly appear right in the place I had just looked without finding it!

Seeking is a process. Jesus says there are areas of life that require more than asking. There must be seeking and searching. Something is lost, hidden from us—and prayer becomes a search, a plea for insight, an intense quest for understanding, a relentless probing and unraveling of the mystery that confronts us.

Again, the answer is absolutely certain. Seek, and you will find!

We have an example of this truth in the well-known incident in the life of the apostle Paul, when he suffered from that painful affliction he called "a thorn in the flesh." It was obviously a physical disability that hounded and limited him—at least he thought it did. Three times he asked to have this "thorn" taken away, but received no answer.

So the apostle realized this was not the kind of thing that is removed by asking; it requires a search.

As he meditated and searched out this thing, waiting upon God, the answer came to him: "My grace is sufficient for you, for my power is made perfect in weakness" (2 Corinthians 12:9). In other words, "It is better this way, Paul. I have allowed this 'thorn' to come into your life, and I will not remove it, for my grace is sufficient for you. I can give you all that it takes to withstand and endure this problem; what it is doing for you is of far more value than anything that would come by its removal."

So Paul concludes in the rest of that verse, "Therefore I will boast all the more gladly about my weaknesses, so that Christ's power may rest on me." Now, what has prayer done in Paul's life? It has broken through the mysterious barrier, the seeming wall of silence, that met the apostle when he asked to have this thing removed. As he prayed about his "thorn in the flesh," the thorn was not removed, but his mind was illuminated. He began to see that, behind his disability, God's purposes were at work.

So, the searching prayer *was* answered. We need not go on in confusion and uncertainty in these perplexing areas of life where God's solution seems long delayed. In such instances the answer is found in seeking. "Seek, and you shall find," Jesus tells us. The answer is absolutely certain.

Level 3: Knock. The third level of prayer is knocking. Here, both time and repetition are involved. Knocking is not a single rap; it is a series of raps. It is a request for admittance, repeated if necessary, and it suggests situations where we seek an entrance or an opportunity. Someone may have erected a barrier against our witness or against our friendship and we are seeking to surmount that barrier, to get behind the wall of resistance, and to have an opportunity freely and openly to speak to or to share in or to enter into a life. That requires knocking.

We may have an unshakable desire to begin a certain type of work or ministry from which we are now excluded. We long to move into that area, and we feel God is leading us, calling us, to be this or to do that. That requires knocking. Perhaps we hunger after knowledge or we hunger after friendship or (as the Word of God says) we hunger and thirst after righteousness. We are looking for an opportunity, seeking entrance into an area that is now restricted from us. This requires knocking. We come before God and boldly and repeatedly ask, each time trying to enter the door of opportunity, because we are confident that what Jesus says here is true, "Knock, and it shall be opened."

We see a remarkable and clear-cut example of knocking in prayer in Paul's letter to the Romans. As he writes to these dear friends, many of whom he had never met but knew by reputation only, he says,

> God, whom I serve with my whole heart in preaching the gospel of his Son, is my witness how constantly I remember you in my prayers at all times; and I pray that now at last by God's will the way may be opened for me to come to you.
>
> I long to see you so that I may impart to you some spiritual gift to make you strong—that is, that you and I may be mutually encouraged by each other's faith (Romans 1:9–12).

Here is an area he wanted to enter into, but he was frustrated again and again. Still, Paul kept trying, knowing that to him who knocks, it shall be opened. And the book of Acts tells us that he finally did reach Rome—though he arrived as a prisoner in chains. God brought Paul to Rome, and from his prison cell in Rome he wrote his "prison epistles," the greatest letters Paul ever wrote.

So prayer is not simply asking. Prayer is also seeking and knocking. The answer, however, is invariably the same, for everyone who asks receives, and he who seeks finds, and to him who knocks it will be opened.

To Him Who Believes

If prayer begins with necessity and moves on to certainty, then it ends on a note of ability: "If you then, though you are evil, know how to give good gifts to your children, how much more will your Father in heaven give the Holy Spirit to those who ask him!" (Luke 11:13).

This is one of the greatly misunderstood passages of Scripture, and it is often taken to refer to the initial indwelling of the Holy Spirit in the human heart. Some people have understood this passage to mean that it is possible to be a Christian and not have the Holy Spirit, and perhaps years after conversion they must ask God for the Spirit to be given to them. But that is not the meaning of the passage at all. Both John and Paul make it explicitly clear that the Spirit of Christ, the Holy Spirit, is received the moment we believe in Jesus Christ.

John's Gospel records that Jesus stood at the last day of the feast and declared, "If anyone is thirsty, let him come to me and drink. Whoever believes in me, as the Scripture has said, streams of living water will flow from within him" (John 7:37–38). And John immediately adds, "By this he meant the Spirit, whom those who believed in him were later to receive. Up to that time the Spirit had not been given, since Jesus had not yet been glorified."

And Paul says, "We were all baptized by one Spirit into one body—whether Jews or Greeks, slave or free" (1 Corinthians 12:13). The Spirit of God does not come by invitation initially. This word about asking for the Spirit is not addressed to unbelievers, but to believers who already have the Holy Spirit!

This is the paradox of Christianity: Though it is true that all Christians have the indwelling Holy Spirit, it is also true (and we are not speaking nonsense when we say this) that we need continually to be filled with the Holy Spirit. That does not mean the Holy Spirit comes in again and again but that we increasingly, daily give ourselves over to His occupancy and His mastery in our lives. All fulfillment of need is then an activity of the Holy Spirit, and that is why Jesus ends this enlightening passage on prayer by reminding us that every Christian is to be continually asking for and receiving that flow of the Spirit's power which alone enables him to do anything in God's sight.

Oswald Chambers, the author of that powerful devotional classic *My Utmost for His Highest* was a philosophy tutor at Dunoon College in England. He was a genuine Christian, no question about it. His faith in Christ as his Savior was sincere and unshakable. But as he lived the Christian life, he came to a deep and troubling conviction that, though he was a genuine Christian, he was an appallingly dull, often defeated, sadly disillusioned Christian. Thinking back over the barrenness of his own spiritual experience, he recorded this reflection: "If this is all there is to Christianity, if I have got all there is, then the thing's a fraud." He became very hungry for something more of God.

Chambers' sense of despair and defeat grew until it reached a crisis in his soul, climaxing at the same time that the great Bible teacher F. B. Meyer was visiting Dunoon College to give a series of sermons. Dr. Meyer was mightily used of God to proclaim the Spirit-filled life, and on this particular occasion he preached from the very verse we are examining: Luke 11:13. Oswald Chambers listened with rapt attention, and he later said that the truth of that verse penetrated his heart with gripping power: "How much more will your Father in heaven give the Holy Spirit to those who ask him!" A brief but fierce battle erupted in his thinking, and at last he simply responded to the verse and said, "Lord, I ask you now for the Holy Spirit and I take Him. I receive Him from you now in faith."

The change that came over Oswald Chambers did not come with wild emotionalism, or a sense of vision, or a feeling of power. It came surely yet quietly and softly, like the whispered assurance of a still, small voice within. Chambers' next step was to talk it all out with a friend. During the conversation, his friend reminded him that Jesus said, "You will receive power when the Holy Spirit comes on you" (Acts 1:8). This is simply a gift from the Lord to be taken, to be accepted, that's all.

"I came to realize," Chambers later recalled, "that God intended me, having asked, to simply take it by faith, and that power would be there." Five years later he recorded the results: "If the previous four years of my life had been nothing but hell on earth, the last five have been heaven on earth. Every aching abyss of my heart has been filled with the overflowing love of God. Love is the beginning, the middle, and the end."

Did that mean the Holy Spirit was not present in Oswald Chambers' heart before he had this experience? Of course not! How else was he a Christian? How else did he realize that Jesus Christ was his, except as the Spirit bore witness with his spirit that he was a child of God?

What happened was that Oswald Chambers surrendered his life to the Holy Spirit to direct his every activity. He accepted the Word of God as sufficient proof that it all would happen as he walked on that promise. And this is what the verse means.

It takes power to live a Christian life. You know that, don't you? It takes power to knock all the self-centeredness out of our lives, and it takes power to keep Christ central in everything. This power does not come by the earnest gritting of our teeth and striving to achieve it. It comes by a continual asking and taking, by a continual praying by faith, "Lord, take me; truly take me, Lord," and then expecting that He has done it. When we do that, God writes upon us the marks of power and sends us out as living epistles to be read and known by all people.

Lord Jesus, we ask that these words may come with fresh and vital meaning to our hearts. Help us to see that there is a grand adventure of your blessing and your power awaiting us as we boldly step out on the basis of your Word alone. Open our eyes to the realization that there are things we need to ask for and take immediately from your hand, other things that we need to seek, and still others for which we need to knock and wait, and knock again. Give us the unshakable assurance that in every case, without any exception, your Word is sure, your answer is true.

As we ask, seek, and knock, we trust you. We know that it will be given. We know that we will find. We expect that it will be opened. Thank you, Lord, for the answer you have promised us.

In Jesus' name, Amen.

7

Praying Together

"I tell you the truth, whatever you bind on earth will be bound in heaven, and whatever you loose on earth will be loosed in heaven.

"Again, I tell you that if two of you on earth agree about anything you ask for, it will be done for you by my Father in heaven. For where two or three come together in my name, there am I with them."

Matthew 18:18–20

"Prayer," someone once observed, "has already divided seas and rolled up flowing rivers, it has made flinty rocks gush into fountains, it has quenched flames of fire, it has muzzled lions, disarmed vipers and poisons, it has marshaled the stars against the wicked, it has stopped the course of the moon and arrested the sun in its race, it has burst open iron gates and recalled souls from eternity, it has conquered the strongest devils and commanded legions of angels down from heaven. Prayer has bridled and chained the raging passions of men and destroyed vast armies of proud, daring, blustering atheists. Prayer has brought one man from the bottom of the sea and carried another in a chariot of fire to heaven."

That is not mere hyperbole. It is historical fact. Prayer is an awesome, mighty force in the world.

So when we read our Lord's words from Matthew 18:18–20, and we begin to glimpse just a hint of their meaning for our lives, we discover a description of prayer that is sobering, even frightening, in its implications. These words reveal both the most attractive and most fearsome thing about prayer—its authority.

Prayer is an awesome thing.

In this passage of Scripture we discover three illuminating insights into prayer from the world's greatest authority on prayer.

Illuminating Insight 1: Binding and Loosing

First, we see that prayer is an authority that operates in mystery: "I tell you the truth, whatever you bind on earth will be bound in heaven, and whatever you loose on earth will be loosed in heaven" (18:18). Binding and loosing. As you read these words, it sounds almost like magic, doesn't it?

Children's fairy tales often include some magic object—a lamp, a ring, or a magic word—with which a person could do the most astonishing things. He could turn people into toads, or cast spells of enchantment or travel by carpet—or even on the wind.

In this one aspect at least, prayer is indeed somewhat like magic. For what our Lord is unquestionably saying here is that quite ordinary humans like you and me have the potential to exercise extraordinary power. He is saying that heaven will in some sense ratify what is done on earth, and that we will connect with a world beyond the commonplace world of our senses.

This is certainly what the Lord means by the way He contrasts heaven and earth in this verse. Surely we must take these words seriously. This does not mean, of course, that prayer is magic or that we can do whatever we fancy—acting by caprice and changing people into all kinds of strange objects. Prayer has limitations, and we will observe these as we go along. But we must grasp the incredible power and the unseen world that we can access through prayer with God the Father.

Reflections of Heaven

Earth, as opposed to heaven, is the world of the senses, the world that demands our attention every day and night. But heaven is not merely future; heaven is also present, and equally as real as earth—you might even say, *more* real than earth! It parallels our familiar physical world, Jesus tells us, and the door between these two worlds is open. The passageway between them is prayer.

Matthew 18:18 points us to the correspondence that exists between heaven and earth. The outer world of time and space and events and history, the world so familiar to us, is but a reflection of that inner, invisible world that surrounds us—God's spiritual kingdom, heaven. In other words, earth is in some sense a reflection of heaven.

With our physical senses we cannot see that inner world. All we see is its reflection in the outer world of history. It is somewhat like the back of your head, which you have never seen. All you can see, at best, is but a reflection of it in a mirror. Then you see the back of your head, not in actuality, but in reflection. You see only the image of it.

In the Christian philosophy of history, the events that are reported in our daily newspapers are simply reflections of what has taken place in the invisible world of spirit—in heaven, if you like—that is within us and around us. And Jesus' amazing statement is that the invisible things that take place in heaven and will be reflected on earth are determined, not in heaven, but on earth in the heart of a praying Christian: "Whatever you bind on earth will be bound in heaven." Whatever we bind in this outward, conscious life of ours, in touch with the things of sense, will be confirmed in that invisible world and will find its reflection again on earth in the things of this life.

Clearly, a mystery is at work here. I do not think any of us can understand exactly why it is that God waits till Christians pray before He begins to do what He has intended all along and even announced that He will do. But it is an indisputable fact that this is exactly what He does. He waits till someone prays before He moves.

We read that when Daniel was an old man, he read in the account of Jeremiah that the Babylonian captivity was about to end, having run the predicted course of seventy years. Daniel was moved to pray mightily that God would send the captives of Israel back to their homeland—and those captives did not begin to return until Daniel prayed!

The principle is also recorded in James 4:2, "You do not have, because you do not ask God." It is that simple. God waits until we ask before He moves.

Our United States government entrusts the president with certain exclusive powers that we could call powers of binding and loosing. Only the president for instance, can sign treaties with foreign powers and thus bind this nation to another. No other individual in our government is authorized to sign a treaty and thus validate it. Only the president can loose the atomic might of this nation. So important is this matter of deciding when to send our great missiles screaming into space that the power to do so has been delegated to one person only, the president of the United States. He has power to veto legislation, to issue executive orders and shape policies and enter into agreements that profoundly effect the lives of every individual in the nation. The citizens might, under certain circumstances, want the president to act in a certain way and might exert tremendous moral force to effect that action, but until he acts, nothing can be done.

Jesus tells us in Matthew 18:18 that God has granted powers of binding and loosing to every believer, and until we act upon them, nothing happens. In the realm of our personal lives these powers are almost absolute. God has said that we have power to bind every form of evil in our own lives. No contrary force can dominate us.

As Paul writes in Romans 6:14, "Sin shall not be your master, because you are not under law, but under grace." By grace we have power to bind every evil force, every contrary authority within us. Paul also tells us that our warfare is not against flesh and blood but is along spiritual lines (see 2 Corinthians 10:3–4). We are warring against evil authorities and powers in high places, and we have power to bring them under control in our own lives as we reckon ourselves dead to sin and alive to God.

Furthermore, we have power to loose the full flood of the Spirit's resources in our own lives. Not one of us has any excuse for not being all that God intends us to be. Someone has well said that we are as victorious as we want to be. No matter what you have been, no matter how weak, how failing, how faltering your life has been, the biblical fact is that you have been exactly as victorious as you have wanted to be. Why? Because power has been granted to us in Jesus Christ to bind every contrary force, every evil motive in our lives, and to loose the flood of the Spirit's power through us—not only in our own lives, but in others as well.

"In others?" you may ask. "How can I have power to bind and loose in the lives of others?" By means of intercessory prayer. Others can be helped tremendously by our prayers. I have often seen young people, in their early Christian experience, drift into apathy and indifference. They become unconcerned about spiritual values, gradually slipping into sin, rebellion, and evil, immoral habits. Then, suddenly, they begin to change—seemingly overnight and without explanation! Their attitudes shift 180 degrees. They begin to grow spiritually. What happened?

Sooner or later it is discovered that someone had become concerned and was praying for that young person. No one may have been at all aware of what was happening, but prayer was changing a life.

As we look at the words in the Scripture text about binding and loosing, we can see that although we do not fully understand what this means, we do know that prayer is the exercise of authority—an authority that operates in mystery. Prayer is the link to that invisible world that is the control center of all human life. We stand on the frontier between two worlds when we pray. Therefore, as James says, "The prayer of a righteous man is powerful and effective" (James 5:16).

Illuminating Insight 2: Authority Expressed in Unity

The second illuminating insight we see in this passage is that the authority of prayer is expressed in unity: "Again, I tell you that if two of you on earth agree about anything you ask for, it will be done for you by my Father in heaven" (Matthew 18:19). This is the charter principle underlying all prayer meetings! One Christian praying alone has great effect, but what happens when two or more gather together? It is evident here that there is an amazing mathematic phenomenon about prayer.

In the Old Testament, Moses told the people of Israel, "How could one man chase a thousand, or two put ten thousand to flight, unless their Rock had sold them, unless the LORD had given them up?" (Deuteronomy 32:30). That is a strange ratio, isn't it? Logic would tell you that if one could chase a thousand, then two would chase two thousand—a remarkable accomplishment by any measure. But spiritual truth transcends mere logic and arithmetic! The Lord says that when two Christians get together and seek God's power, there is an exponential increase in the effect of their prayers! Two shall put not two thousand, but *ten thousand* to flight!

From the earliest days of the church, believers have sensed the need to gather together in prayer. In the fourth chapter of Acts we see the church gathered for prayer after they had been persecuted by the Sanhedrin. Acts 12 reports another such instance: when the church met and prayed for Peter, and he was delivered from prison. They could hardly believe it, but it was true. This is corporate prayer. What is the purpose of prayer like this? Jesus says it is that we might agree together: "If two of you on earth agree about anything you ask for, it will be done for you by my Father in heaven."

Words are fascinating things. There are at least eight words in the Greek New Testament that are translated *agree*. One of them means literally "to stand together." It means two people make a common decision.

But we have to be very careful about the assumptions we make when we interpret Scripture—especially when it comes to the issue of prayer. Many people have misunderstood this verse, thinking it means that if a person wants something, he finds someone else who wants the same thing. Then they agree on it in prayer, and God must honor their prayer and do their will. This misinterpretation of Scripture portrays God as someone less than God, less than Lord—it characterizes Him as nothing more than a genie in a bottle, who is forced to do human bidding if humans find the key to manipulate Him! That is not what this verse means at all!

Agree, as the word is used here, means "to sound together, to harmonize." Two particular notes struck on a piano will harmonize. But the harmony is already there, it is simply brought out as you strike the right notes. It is as if God has already written the musical score, and it remains only for two Christians to come together and play the duet according to the notes God has already written! That is genuine harmony and agreement!

When believers agree, one says what is on his heart, what he believes God wants him to pray for, what he has found to be in accordance with God's will as expressed in Scripture and in the leading of the Holy Spirit. The other believer agrees, saying what is on his heart, what he believes God wants him to pray for after also searching God's Word and his own sense of the Spirit's leading. Where they find they agree, where they harmonize, are the areas where they can fully expect God to work. God says, "It shall be done."

That is a glorious definiteness, isn't it? It shall be done! This is why I like to hear people say "Amen!" at prayer meetings. I am old-fashioned enough to enjoy hearing a good "Amen" now and then—and, after all, that is exactly what the Scriptures suggest. When one person is leading in prayer, everyone else is listening (or ought to be!), and when something is said that strikes a responsive chord, they say "Amen," either silently or vocally. What they are really saying is, "I agree; this is what God has said to me, too."

When amens are sprinkled throughout a prayer meeting, either vocally or silently, it marks the areas of firm agreement where the Spirit of God is at work bringing unity. This is where prayer finds its authority.

Over the years, in the church I pastored, the board of elders learned that the mind of the Spirit is revealed when all fourteen elders meeting together are united. When they feel there is unity, they feel God's will has been discovered. This is what Jesus is conveying to us: "Where two or three of you sound the same note—not by comparing notes beforehand, but by hearing God's harmonic chord within you, individually and collectively—it will be done by my Father in heaven."

Moreover, it is evident in verse 20 that prayer is also an authority that originates in personality: "For where two or three come together in my name, there am I with them." Don't miss the force of that little introductory word *For.* Here is the explanation of the mystery in verse 18.

I confess that I do not fully understand how it is that a man or woman, boy or girl, praying on the basis of the binding and loosing powers granted by God, can move such mighty forces—the forces that called the universe into existence. But, of course, it is not merely a human being praying, but also Christ living in that human being who prays through that human being's prayers. "It is God who works in you to will and to act according to his good purpose" (Philippians 2:13).

Now you can see how clearly this reveals that Christians are creatures of two worlds. In our humanity, like everyone else of the human race, we belong to earth. We live in a world of space and time, touching the events around us and reacting to them as others do. We read the same newspapers, hear the same television reports, and are subject to the same pressures as all the other worldlings around us. We are creatures of earth.

But in the new life in Jesus Christ, in the heavenlies where we live in Christ, we are creatures of heaven and are in touch with the invisible world—the world that controls the outer world. We are standing on the frontier between those two worlds. As someone has well put it, our prayers could truly be pictured as the act of God the Son praying to God the Father by the power of God the Spirit in the prayer room of the believer's heart. That is the whole story of prayer.

Illuminating Insight 3: Jesus, the Source of Our Unity

The indwelling personality of Jesus Christ is not only the explanation of the mystery of the power of prayer, but is also the source of the unity we have talked about. In writing to the Ephesians, Paul said that Jesus Christ is far above all rule and authority, power and dominion, and every title that can be given, not only in the present age but also in the one to come. And God placed all things under his feet and appointed him to be head over everything for the church, which is his body, the fullness of him who fills everything in every way (Ephesians 1:21–23).

In other words, the expression of the power of Jesus Christ is never fully seen in an individual Christian, but only in the church as a whole. The simplest form of the church is described by our Lord as wherever "two or three come together in my name." You and I as individual Christians cannot fully reflect Jesus Christ. It is only when two or three—or two or three hundred or two or three thousand—are gathered together in His name that all the power that is Christ's is fully manifested in this life. This means we can never fully know Jesus Christ unless we know Him in relation to someone else. In Ephesians 3:18–19 Paul prays that we

may have power, together with all the saints, to grasp how wide and long and high and deep is the love of Christ, and to know this love that surpasses knowledge—that you may be filled to the measure of all the fullness of God.

Notice especially that phrase, "together with all the saints." The power Paul describes comes to us collectively whenever and wherever two or three or more are gathered in Christ's name. We will never know it by ourselves. We can take God's Word and study it by ourselves, we can analyze it and saturate our minds with it and memorize it, but until we begin to share it with other Christians, we can never grasp who Jesus Christ fully is. Furthermore, we can never learn how mighty and glorious He is unless we begin to make demands upon His inexhaustible power and His glory.

Don't miss this: Jesus says, "where two or three are gathered together in my name." The wisdom of this world says, "There is strength in numbers." Jesus says, in effect, "There is strength in my name—and as few as two or three people, gathered together in my name, are sufficient to access that strength."

The power of the church does not lie in the numbers that it can gather together, in mass movements, mass events, mass communication of the gospel. Yes, God can and does use great numbers—such as in a Billy Graham evangelistic crusade or a Luis Palau broadcast—but the strength of the church is not in the numbers, it is in the Lord Himself. Some people seem to think that if we can just get enough people together to pray and act and get involved in a mass way, we will have enough power to correct the things that are wrong in the world and set them right again. Nothing could be further from the truth.

Another misconception is that the power of the church is determined by its status in a community. We seem to think that if we can draw into the church people who are in positions of authority or leadership or stature in the community, we will have enough status to wield great power in the minds and hearts of men and women. How foolish we are! The power of the church does not rest in its numbers, its status, its wealth, its money, its position. The power of the church of Jesus Christ is stated right here, "Where two or three come together in my name, there am I with them."

Out of Jesus alone flows this marvelous power to bind and to loose, and from His personality and being alone comes this tremendous unity by which the mind of the Spirit becomes known, so that God can move through Christian lives to alter the destiny of the world. Let us glory in that! If we wish to glory in anything, let us glory (as the early church did) in the fact that Jesus Christ lives and moves in our midst, that we belong to Him, and that His life is expressed through us. It is only through Him that prayer makes its greatest, permanent impact. It is only through His presence that prayer has meaning and value.

Father, what a mistake we make when we take the profound truths that your Son has presented to us so simply, and try to make them complex. How wonderful it is to come back to the sincerity and clarity that is in Jesus Christ. How foolish we are to seek substitutes for your simple truths and for that simple, attainable relationship between the God of the universe and two or three united believers, joined in the simple act of prayer.

Lord, teach us to glory in this, teach us to reckon upon it, teach us to pray on this basis and this alone. And, having recognized that the things you have taught us are true, regardless of what the circumstances around us may be, grant us the faith to step out upon them and act upon them, boldly and confidently in the name of your Son, Jesus.

For it is in His name we pray, Amen.

8

The Holy Spirit and Prayer

"I tell you the truth, anyone who has faith in me will do what I have been doing. He will do even greater things than these, because I am going to the Father. And I will do whatever you ask in my name, so that the Son may bring glory to the Father. You may ask me for anything in my name, and I will do it.

"If you love me, you will obey what I command. And I will ask the Father, and he will give you another Counselor to be with you forever—the Spirit of truth. The world cannot accept him, because it neither sees him nor knows him. But you know him, for he lives with you and will be in you. I will not leave you as orphans; I will come to you."

John 14:12–18

In 1930, King George of England was set to make history by addressing an international arms control summit in London—an event made historic by the fact that the speech would be broadcast around the world by the first worldwide radio linkup ever attempted. The speech would be carried live in the United States by the Columbia Broadcasting System (CBS). Just moments before the king began to speak, however, a technician tripped over a cable in the New York studio, causing the connection to be broken. The cable was not simply unplugged—it was severed.

The CBS chief engineer, a man named Harold Vidian, looked around for a piece of cable to patch the connection, but none was available. So he did the only thing he could do. He took one end of the severed connection in one hand and the other end in the other hand. As he closed the circuit with his own flesh, the distant signal from England could suddenly be heard.

The king of England began to speak to the world over the radio. People in the United States who heard the king were indebted to Harold Vidian, who willingly endured the pain of maintaining the connection for over half an hour as several hundred volts of electric current zapped through his body. The king's message was carried to the people through a power that coursed through a single human being.

In a similar way, we help broadcast the message of our king—King Jesus!—when we make ourselves available to the power that seeks to course through us and electrify us and make us channels for Him. The electrifying power of God comes to us as we invite His Spirit to enter us and move through us and activate us. And we cannot fully understand what it means to pray until we understand the role of the Holy Spirit in the process of prayer.

Three Revelations

Jesus never taught His disciples how to preach. He taught them how to *pray*. Much of His teaching on prayer is found in the rich and fragrant passage in the gospel of John, the Upper Room Discourse. This passage is one of the most challenging sections of Scripture. Great mystery, beauty, and glory are found in these verses. In this passage, perhaps more than anywhere else in the Bible, our Lord unfolds the unique secret of Christianity, the aspect of life that has been called "the exchanged life."

This is the secret of being an effective Christian. We do not live our own lives. We live the life of another—or, more accurately, another lives His life through us. Until we grasp that as the key to the mystery of Christian living, we have not graduated from the kindergarten level of the Christian life.

In this chapter in our study, we will relate the subject of prayer to the total spectrum of Christian living. No passage of Scripture more practically or effectively instructs us in the workings of prayer than John 14. In verses 12 through 17, we discover three profound revelations regarding the life of Jesus Christ that are at work within us. In verse 12 we learn that the character of a Christian's work is *borrowed activity*. In verses 13 and 14 we find that the basis of a Christian's prayer is *borrowed authority;* and in verses 15 through 17 we discover that the secret of Christian living is *borrowed deity*. Let's explore each of these three profound revelations in detail.

Revelation 1: Borrowed Activity

Each of these divisions consists of a staggering promise of tremendous potential, but we must see that each promise is linked with a qualifying condition.

Frequently as we read these great passages of the Scripture, we are either so dazzled by the promise that we fail to heed the condition, or we are so frightened by the condition that we pay little heed to the promise. But it is necessary that we take very seriously both aspects of what our Lord has said.

Perhaps our greatest problem is that we are often so awe-struck by these promises that we fail to heed the condition. You've seen this statement: when all else fails, follow directions. Sometimes when we try to lay hold of a promise of God and it does not appear to work, the reason is that we have not followed the directions related to the promise. Thus, a conditioning statement is always the road to fulfillment.

In verse 12, the promise is staggering in its implications. There, Jesus tells us about the work we will do in His name—a work that could be called *borrowed activity:*

> "I tell you the truth, anyone who has faith in me will do what I have been doing. He will do even greater things than these, because I am going to the Father."

Although we might accept what Jesus is saying here on a theoretical basis, we find that, practically speaking, His promise is unbelievable. We refuse to accept it at face value. We feel there must be a catch somewhere. Is Jesus really saying that Christians living today, at the threshold of the third millennium, can do not only the works that Jesus did, but also greater works than these?

The promise is so overwhelming that we immediately attempt to soften it. We say to ourselves, "Can this be true of me? After all, I am not Jesus Christ, and I can't be expected to do what He did!" But how do you square an excuse like that with a verse like this? For that is precisely what Jesus plainly says!

Here is where we need to carefully observe exactly what Jesus is saying. He is not saying here that a sincere, dedicated Christian of today will actually be able, in his sincerity and his dedicated religious effort, to do what Jesus did in the first century. Jesus is not comparing our labors now with His labors then. He is not saying that dedicated Christian men and women are really going to transcend what He accomplished as the Son of God incarnate.

What Jesus *is* saying is this: *The risen Christ will do through us greater works than He did as the incarnate Christ living among men!* Do you see the difference? That's an incredible promise—but it makes absolute biblical sense. It is not we but He who will do these greater works—and He will perform them through us. It is not our activity that makes a difference in the world, it is *borrowed activity*—work that we borrow from Christ, and which He performs on earth through us.

Notice what He links with this: "Because I am going to the Father." What does He mean? Simply this: His going to the Father released the full potential of the Godhead for human lives and events. While He was here on earth, the fullness of God was available to man only in one human body, the body of Jesus Christ. By the strength and indwelling life of the Father He did all the works that we marvel at as we read the story of His life. But what He is saying now is that, as the risen Christ, ascended to the throne of the Father, He Himself will do through us. He will accomplish this in terms of our personalities and by the activity of our lives, and what He accomplishes through us today will be greater works than He did in the days when He lived in the flesh on earth.

A Complete Failure

It is rather startling to realize that the work of the incarnate Christ—that is, Jesus Christ of Nazareth working and walking among men—was, at its end, apparently a total and complete failure. We marvel as we read the story of the beginning of His ministry. He performed astonishing miracles—raising the dead; healing the sick; opening the eyes of the blind; delivering men, women, and little children from the oppression of demons; touching with His hand the withered arm of a man and restoring it immediately to full growth and life again.

And we read the tremendous words that came from His lips—the Sermon on the Mount; the parables beside the seashore; the countless mysterious, marvelous, and compelling things He said. It is no wonder that crowds followed Him, hounding Him, following Him even into retreat, insisting upon His ministry. Indeed, it is not surprising that the news spread like wildfire that a prophet had risen in Israel again. Men left their work and their cities and their ordinary activities of life and went out to hear what He had to say, following Him for hours on end. That was the beginning.

But at the end, where were the crowds? They had been diminishing for quite some time: "From this time many of his disciples turned back and no longer followed him" (John 6:66). Already many of the searching things He had been saying had separated the weak from the strong, and toward the end of His ministry the actual number of disciples had been reduced to a handful. And even these, in the hour of His capture and appearance before Pilate, forsook Him and fled. In His time of need they left Him. A tiny band of only one man and three or four women gathered around the foot of the cross. That was all the incarnate

Christ had to show for the marvelous ministry in the power of the Spirit He had manifested among people.

A total failure! That is the value of the works He did. Now do you see what He means when He says we will do "even greater things than these" because He is going to the Father? As a man, His ministry among men was a failure. It did not remain; it had no enduring effects. Those who came, attracted by the things they saw, faded back into the shadows when persecution began to grow. No one stayed with Him.

But a very significant promise is given in the midst of this Upper Room Discourse when Jesus says to His disciples, "You did not choose me, but I chose you and appointed you to go and bear fruit—fruit that will last. Then the Father will give you whatever you ask in my name" (John 15:16). Your fruit should remain. What you do in the power of the Spirit will not fade away. Those whom you win to Christ will abide. Christ's cause will flourish on the earth and spread to the uttermost parts till every nation hears the word, and out of every tribe and nation of earth will come, at last, fruit that will remain.

This is what Jesus meant when He said that we "will do even greater things than these, because I am going to the Father." It is His work in us. A Christian's true work is borrowed activity. It is never our own, and when we begin to think it is, we defeat every possibility of success. We sabotage the work of the Holy Spirit.

But note that a condition is involved here. What is it? "Anyone who has faith in me." That is the condition. And without fulfillment of that condition, the promise will never be fulfilled in our lives.

Notice that Jesus did not say, "Anyone who is a Christian." And I think for good reason. Many people classify themselves as believers because at some time in their lives they received Jesus Christ in their hearts as Lord and Savior. That is not the meaning here at all. Jesus is using a verb here in the present tense which means, "The person who continually believes in me."

Only the person who continually appropriates by faith all that Jesus is, will do the things He does—or rather, will experience the life of Jesus living and working through him or her. In the Christian life, *faith* is always the operative word. Jesus is not saying that the person who *holds* the truth will do these works, but the person who *acts* upon the truth. God gives power and ability only to faith, and it is only when we learn this that these promises come alive.

Although we know these promises must be true because of Him who spoke them, we see so little evidence of their truth in our lives simply because we are not ready to take God at His word, expecting Him to do great things. Only through an expectant attitude of faith are these promises realized.

Revelation 2: Borrowed Authority

Just as the basis of a Christian's work is borrowed activity, so the basis of a Christian's prayer is *borrowed authority:*

> "I will do whatever you ask in my name, so that the Son may bring glory to the Father. You may ask me for any-thing in my name, and I will do it" (John 14:13–14).

That is a breathtaking statement: "Whatever you ask . . . anything in my name . . . I will do it." This promise is so amazing that we immediately suspect a catch. This promise sounds too broad and unconditional. If we take this as absolutely unlimited, a sort of magical Aladdin's lamp that we can rub and ask for anything in the world, then certainly we have missed the true point of this passage.

We sense also, almost instinctively, that conflicts would immediately arise if no limits accompanied the promise. We can see problems arising. What if a Christian athlete is praying for clear weather and a Christian farmer is praying for rain? Who wins?

No, this promise cannot be limitless; it is conditional. Our Lord means exactly what He says, but it is essential that we understand precisely what He means. This is a magnificent promise of vast scope, of tremendous encompassment, but we dare not miss the real implications of that all-important, twice-stated clause, "in my name." This is the condition.

Many of us think of the phrase "in Jesus' name, Amen," almost as a magical formula to be tacked on to the end of our prayers. Nothing is quite as pagan or silly as adding a phrase of mumbo-jumbo to our prayers without any understanding of what the phrase means.

To truly ask something of God the Father in Jesus' name is not mumbo-jumbo. It is not just a closing phrase like appending "Sincerely yours" at the end of a letter. To pray in the name of Jesus has a very specific significance that has become lost to many Christians over the years because of our tendency to practice churchianity rather than Christianity. We pray our formalized, ritualized prayers, using certain formulas simply because that's the way it has always been done. We have failed to look freshly and think deeply about what it really means to pray in the name of Jesus.

To ask something in Christ's name means to ask *by His authority*. It means to ask on the basis of His character, according to the merit of His work, and by the power and right that He has personally given to us. It means that Jesus has lent His authority to us, giving us the right to pray according to His authority, which we have borrowed.

We are all familiar with the phrase, "In the name of the law." Law enforcement does its business in the name of the law. Suppose a police officer is sent into a dangerous slum area of the city at three o'clock in the afternoon, responding to a call of a violent crime in progress. When he arrives at the designated address, he knocks at the door and calls out, "Open in the name of the law." After knocking repeatedly without getting an answer, he draws his gun, kicks down the door, and makes his arrest.

Now, let's shift the scene to later that night, possibly ten o'clock. That same officer is passing through a residential area, only now he's off duty and is staggering drunk. In a belligerent attitude he stumbles up the steps of a house, knocks on the door, and shouts, "Open in the name of the law." The people inside hear the commotion and realize there's a drunk at the door, so they refuse to open up. In a rage the off-duty officer breaks down the door, and when he does, the police are called, he is arrested, and taken to jail.

What's the difference between the two events? It is the same policeman carrying out the same actions. Even the words are the same: "In the name of the law." But the action in the afternoon was truly carried out in the name of the law, while the scene at night was done outside the law—despite the use of that phrase. One was authorized activity, the other was unauthorized. That is what Jesus means when He says "In my name." The issue is one of *authority*.

When we ask anything in Jesus' name, we are to ask within the realm and scope of His work, His character, and His will. Whatever He is interested in accomplishing on earth, we, as the instruments of His activity, are involved in accomplishing it and must be in alignment with His plan. "Whatever you need to carry out my will, to accomplish my plan, under the umbrella of my authority," He says in effect, "just ask for it and it will be done." Whatever! Anything! If it is a need within this scope of His authority and plan, we can ask for it and it will be done without fail.

I was once asked to give a talk at a breakfast in Newport Beach, California. As is often the case, I felt very inadequate for the task. The meeting was held in lavish surroundings at an affluent resort area where great religious indifference was likely to abound. I knew that the gathering would include scores of men who did not identify themselves as Christians—and in fact, many of them would be typically shallow, rootless modern pagans. It was a challenging situation, an opportunity to speak in the name of God to men who would otherwise never give an ear. I felt the tremendous challenge and my own inability.

I have learned by long experience and by the Word of God to recognize such feelings of inadequacy as a good sign. I welcome those feelings now, because I know they are designed to lead me to ask for the help I need. So, before the meeting began, I asked God for three things: (1) that what I said might be relevant to the lives of these people; (2) that my words might be challenging and would awaken them to God's truth; and (3) that God's message might be powerful, and would penetrate human hearts—even hardened hearts—with power.

What I said that morning was neither clever nor profound. Actually, it was very simple. I merely tried to call attention to the moral revolt that is widespread in the United States today and the fact that it is eating away at our national life and destroying the very foundation of our gov-ernment and society—certainly not a new or startling mes-sage. I pointed out something of the moral emptiness of such a way of life, and described how futile and meaningless this kind of life seems to be, and what the Christian answer is.

Immediately after the meeting, two police chiefs from the cities of Newport Beach and Costa Mesa came up to me, visibly moved. They shook my hand and said, "We know what you are talking about. This is the first time we have ever heard anything that seems to suggest an answer. This is what we desperately need down in this area." Next, the mayor of a nearby community (whom I learned had once insisted he would have nothing to do with this meet-ing), came to me and said he felt I had sounded out the cry-ing need of that area and he hoped this would be an annual event. He welcomed our ministry team to come down the next week and hold breakfast meetings throughout Southern California.

How do you explain that? I can suggest only one explanation: "Whatever you ask in my name . . . anything in my name . . . I will do it." That's it! That's the answer! If you ask for anything that furthers the plan and will of Jesus Christ in the affairs of this world, then whatever you ask, anything at all, it will be given. Anything!

The goal of Jesus is to "bring glory to the Father" through us, by lending His authority to us. By His bor-rowed authority, in His name, in alignment with His will, we can ask anything and He will do it.

Revelation 3: Borrowed Deity

In verses 15 through 17, we discover the fact that the secret of the Christian's life is *borrowed deity*. There, Jesus tells us,

"If you love me, you will obey what I command. And I will ask the Father, and he will give you another Counselor to be with you forever—the Spirit of truth. The world cannot accept him, because it neither sees him nor knows him. But you know him, for he lives with you and will be in you."

What a staggering promise! Our Lord tells us that the One who will come to make His home in every Christian's heart and life is no one less than God Himself! The One who comes is the third person of the Trinity, who supplies to us the fullness of God.

The names Jesus uses in John 14:15–17 suggest the richness of this promise. He says that the Spirit will be "another Counselor." I like the old translation better—"Comforter"—but we should understand the word in its original meaning. It comes from the word *fortis*, which means "to make strong" and *com*, which means "with." A comforter is one who stands with you and makes you strong—one who gives strength. In using this word, Jesus is saying first of all that He who comes will be the One who has within Him the fullness of power, all the strength that we could possibly need.

Then He is called "the Spirit of truth," and that is a wonderful statement. Don't you hunger after truth sometimes? In this bewildering world, this perplexing age in which we live, don't you sometimes almost physically hunger for someone, somewhere, somehow, who can tell you the truth? Well, that is who this One is, the Spirit of truth, the One who unfolds reality, who exposes error, who tears away the veils, who dissolves the mists that confuse and blind us, who removes the doubts and brings us face-to-face with things as they really are in life.

I read a wonderful testimony by Dr. Emile Caillet about his discovery of the Bible. At the age of twenty-one he had never even seen a Bible, and it wasn't until years later as a married man that he was finally given one. He began to read it and discovered that this was the answer to his lifelong search for what he called "a book that understands me." As he read, he discovered that this book revealed the One who understood him. The Spirit of truth, who authored the book, told him the truth about himself.

Note, this privilege is exclusively Christian. Only the Christian can be led by the Spirit of God into the nature of reality, into truth. Jesus said of the Spirit of truth that the people of this world "cannot accept him, because it neither sees him nor knows him. But you know him, for he lives with you and will be in you." The Spirit of truth is for Christians only. The world will never be able to understand reality! As long as human beings remain worldlings, they are blinded to the ultimate nature of things. They will never understand them because humanity is both the specimen to be examined and the examiner—and the error that is in the examiner affects the examination! Human beings reason continually in a vicious circle of unbelief that prevents them from discovering ultimate reality.

But when the Spirit of truth comes, He takes away the veils, He dissolves the mists. Little by little, gradually, we begin to understand who we are, and what we are, and why we are what we are, and why others are what they are, and what this world is and where it is going and what its end is going to be. The Spirit of truth reveals these things. Nothing is more magnificently Christian than this ability to see truth clearly.

Now we come to the condition—for the brutal fact is, that though every true Christian has the Spirit of truth living within, many Christians walk in darkness and under-stand no more about themselves than the blindest pagan. Though we have the Spirit available to us, we can be as deluded and as blinded as any worldling living next door. Though we have the potential that the worldling does not have, we may choose not to realize that potential. We may be Bible-taught, but not necessarily Spirit-taught.

Why? Because Jesus says, "He lives with you and will be in you," and there is a vital distinction in these words. Now, I know as well as you do that every believer, when he receives Jesus Christ, receives the indwelling Spirit of God. We do not need to pray again for His coming. He is there right from the start. Historically it was true that these dis-ciples were not to receive the indwelling of the Spirit until the Day of Pentecost. He dwelt with them before, but He was to be in them on the Day of Pentecost.

But, having said all that, it is still true that though the Spirit of God dwells positionally in you, as far as you are concerned, it is as though He only dwelt with you. He has taken up a *position* with you but does not have full *possession* of you! You are not laying hold of His indwelling life, and for all practical purposes He is not in you but only with you. He is fully available to you, but you have not "borrowed" Him. This is the explanation for the prevailing weakness in Christian living. This is the principle of *borrowed deity*.

A group of us once wrestled with this problem, and one of the young men who was with us said a very helpful and insightful thing: "You know, I think I know what the problem is. I have found in my own life that when I simply gave up arguing with the Lord and started obeying Him, all these things begin to work. In my experience I have discov-ered it is possible to have God at arm's length, even though

He is dwelling with me. And when He is out there, nothing works. But when I yield to His sovereign direction in my life and begin to act on what He says, then He is in me and things begin to happen."

He put his finger right on the issue. "In you" means that you are under the control of the Holy Spirit and yielding obedience to His rightful sovereignty. It means the total collapse of all your rebellion against Him.

"Oh," you say, "I'm not in rebellion against the Spirit of God! I'm a Christian! I don't rebel against Him!" In response let me ask you: What kind of life are you living? Is it God-centered or self-centered? Are your activities and your desires aimed at pleasing yourself or pleasing Him? If you are focused primarily on pleasing yourself, then you are in rebellion against the Spirit of God. To have Him dwelling in you means the total collapse of all revolt, and you can say, "Lord Jesus, your Word is my command, I am ready to obey."

It is not our relationship with Jesus Christ that counts before the world. It is our resemblance to Him that the world longs to see. As we allow the Spirit of truth to course through us, to electrify our lives, to empower our actions, the world will see how we live—and the world will want what we have. As we live by the threefold principle of borrowed activity, borrowed authority, and borrowed deity, our lives will become aligned with God's, and our prayers will be answered by God with a resounding "Yes!"

God, search our own hearts! Save us from the self-delusion of talking truth while living a lie. Save us from the hypocrisy of echoing orthodoxy but refusing to submit our lives, day by day and hour by hour, to your eternal will and purpose. Align our lives with your eternal life.

Teach us to act out your activity, borrowed only from you. Teach us to pray by your authority, borrowed only from you. Fill us with yourself, your Spirit of truth, your personality, borrowed only from you. Help us to make ourselves fully available to you in prayer and in daily action, so that we may know the fullness of the glory of these promises fulfilled in our lives.

We ask all of this in Jesus' name, Amen.

Part Three

Jesus faces the shadow of the cross as He prays aloud for His disciples, but there is not one word of fear—only an awareness of anticipated opportunity. The hour has come in which all that He had lived for would begin to be fulfilled. He asks to be restored to the place of glory which He enjoyed with the Father before the world was made. While on earth, He had continually laid aside His own glory, emptying Himself in order that God might be glorified.

This must also be our prayer, for anything less yields nothing but frustration and defeat. While Jesus prays for the Father to keep us in the life-giving relationship with Him, He makes it clear that our part—both the easiest and hardest thing in the world—is simply to believe the truth.

We will never go any farther than our faith takes us. But the Father is also aiming beyond us. His ultimate target is the entire world, and we must become part of the process of drawing a struggling, rebellious creation to Himself.

9

The True Lord's Prayer

After Jesus said this, he looked toward heaven and prayed: "Father, the time has come. Glorify your Son, that your Son may glorify you. For you granted him authority over all people that he might give eternal life to all those you have given him. Now this is eternal life: that they may know you, the only true God, and Jesus Christ, whom you have sent."

John 17:1–3

129

If a number of Christians were asked to repeat the Lord's Prayer, most would begin, "Our Father which art in heaven," for this is universally called "The Lord's Prayer." Actually, though, it is not the Lord's Prayer at all; it is the disciples' prayer. It is the prayer the Lord gave us as a model for our own prayer life.

The true Lord's Prayer—the prayer He prayed shortly before going to the cross—is found in John 17. It has been called "the Holy of Holies of the New Testament," for here, in the shadow of the cross, our Lord gathers with His disciples in the Upper Room. In their presence He prays to the Father.

I never read this passage without a sense of awe and reverence—yet with too much awe and reverence may come a danger. If we habitually approach this passage with a sense of its majesty and beauty, we may miss the Lord's message out of a reluctance to explore in depth what our Lord is truly saying.

If this has been your experience, as I confess it has been mine, the very purpose our Lord envisioned when He prayed this prayer has been defeated. He deliberately prayed aloud in the presence of His disciples because He wanted them to hear what He said. The basic relationship He expresses in this prayer between Himself and the Father is also the relationship that ought to exist between Jesus and us. There is a very real sense in which every believer in Jesus Christ can pray this prayer, for it was designed to teach us how to pray.

The Shadow of the Cross

The first three verses of this prayer set forth the background out of which the prayer arises—a background of danger and death. It was uttered just a few moments before

Jesus left the Upper Room and, with His disciples, went down into the dark valley of the Kidron. And continuing across onto the slopes of the Mount of Olives, He found His way in the darkness of night into the Garden of Gethsemane. There, withdrawing a short distance from the disciples, He prayed a second, desperate prayer which wrung the very blood from His body, so that it fell in great, anguished droplets to the ground. To that garden, Judas came with the guards who took Him prisoner and led Him to Pilate's judgment hall and to the cross.

So Jesus faces the shadow of the cross when He prays this prayer in the Upper Room. The disciples are subdued and terrified. They sense that something is wrong. He has told them He is leaving, and their hearts are wrenched with fear and anxiety. But in His prayer there is not one word of fear.

I have in my library a copy of the prayer that Martin Luther uttered before he appeared before the Emperor of the Holy Roman Empire in the city of Worms to answer the charges against him. It is a prayer he offered knowing that his very life was at stake. In this long, rambling cry to God, Luther confesses his weakness and casts himself again and again upon God for strength and help.

But this prayer of Jesus is entirely different. Instead of a cry of weakness or a plea for help, the prayer begins with a powerful awareness of anticipated opportunity: "After Jesus said this, he looked toward heaven and prayed: 'Father, the time has come. Glorify your Son, that your Son may glorify you' " (John 17:1). With these words Jesus looks forward with obvious anticipation to a time of boundless opportunity that lies before Him. Surely these words, *the time has come,* mean a good deal more than the phrase we employ when we face the end of life, "My time has come."

By that we mean we have come to the end of our rope, the end of life.

From a purely human perspective, a phrase like "my time has come" is a statement of resignation—but what Jesus is speaking of here is realization, not resignation. This is the hour He has been looking forward to all His life, the hour to which He continually refers throughout the record of the Gospels.

In the beginning of John we have the story of the first miracle in Cana of Galilee when Jesus turned the water into wine. There His mother came to Him and said, "They have no more wine," and His answer was, "Dear woman, why do you involve me? My time has not yet come" (John 2:3–4). He meant that even though He would perform what His mother had suggested, it would not have the results she anticipated, for the hour had not yet come. Again and again He said to the disciples, "My hour is not yet." But now, as He approaches the cross, He lifts His eyes to the heavens and says, "Father, the time has come." By this He means the hour in which all He had lived for would begin to be fulfilled.

A Grain of Wheat

This anticipation was based upon the principle, as He once put it, "I tell you the truth, unless a kernel of wheat falls to the ground and dies, it remains only a single seed. But if it dies, it produces many seeds" (John 12:24). This is why His hour had not come before: Jesus knew that God's work is never accomplished apart from the principle of death. All the mighty miracles He did and the mighty words He spoke—all the marvelous power of His ministry in the world—would be totally ineffective until He had passed through the experience of giving up all that He was.

Until that was accomplished, nothing lasting would remain.

Beyond the cross, Jesus knew, lay the glory of God. In Hebrews we read that He endured the cross, despising the shame of it, knowing that beyond it lay the joy which He awaited. Beyond the cross lies glory, but the only way to glory is through the cross. All of His ministry, all of His life, would be ineffective until He had fulfilled this principle of death.

Unless a grain of wheat dies it abides alone: It will never do anything else. It cannot! Only if it dies does it bring forth fruit. Beyond the surrender of His rights lay the possession of privilege; beyond the obedient act was the realized blessing.

This is why we also must pray this prayer, for we are always coming to hours like this in our lives. In both minor and major ways, we come to the place where we must say, "Father, the time has come—the time where I must make a choice as to whether I shall hold my life for myself, to act in self-centeredness as I have been doing all along, or whether I shall fling it away and, passing into apparent death, lay hold of the hope and glory that lies beyond."

Such hours come to all of us. We call them disappointments, setbacks, tragedies, losses. We think of them as injustices, invasions of our privacy, assaults on our right to live our own lives. But if we see them as Jesus saw them, we will recognize that each moment like this is an hour of great possibility. If we will act on the principle of giving ourselves away, we shall discover an open door to an unimaginable realm of service, blessing, and glory. That is what Jesus means when He says, "The time has come." It was a time of abounding opportunity.

Power Over All Flesh

Then our Lord continues His prayer: "Glorify your Son, that your Son may glorify you. For you granted him authority over all people that he might give eternal life to all those you have given him" (John 17:1–2). Here is the revelation that He is aware of an adequate relationship. If you look at that text very carefully, you will notice a marvelous interplay of personality. The Father gives to the Son in order that the Son may give back to the Father. It is not a once-for-all giving in which the Father once gave the Son power over all flesh, but it is a continuous giving.

The Father, Jesus says, is continually giving power over all flesh to the Son. Why? In order that the Son may continually give back to the Father the men whom the Father gives to Him that they may be His. And what He expresses here in this marvelous language is simply that His entire ministry is a manifestation of adequate power for any demand.

The Father gave Jesus power. For what purpose? In order, Jesus says, to give eternal life to whomever the Father has given Him—in order to meet the need of any who come to Him. Those who are sent of the Father, drawn by the Father, shall come to Jesus. Whoever it may be, the Father has given Jesus everything that is necessary to meet the needs of that person. The Son is equal to any problem, whatever it may be.

I was once at a social gathering in a beautiful home when a man came up to me, seized my hand, and said, "I need to talk with you. I've been listening to the message series you've been giving, and I want to ask you some questions." There were lines of deep tragedy in his face. As he spoke, I learned that his seventeen-year-old son had committed suicide just a few months earlier—a devastating event for himself and his wife. As we talked, he said, "I know I have heard something in your messages and in the testimonies of other Christians that must be an answer. I cannot deny that what I have been hearing is real. There is something here, and I want this. I want to come to Christ, but I cannot come."

"Why not?" I asked.

"Because," he responded, "I do not feel I can come until I can come in complete honesty. I have a great deal of doubt, as well as resentment and bitterness about what has happened to us. I just don't think I can come."

"Friend," I said to him, "if you don't feel you can come honestly, then come dishonestly and tell Christ so, for the invitation of the gospel is, 'Whosoever will, let him come.' That's all, 'let him come.' "

There is in Jesus Christ an adequate answer to any problem. You don't have the answer, but you don't need to. He has the answer. Bring the problem to Him, whatever it may be: doubt, unbelief, dishonesty, fear, bitterness, anxiety, worry, whatever it is. Remember Jesus said, "Come to me, all you who are weary and burdened, and I will give you rest" (Matthew 11:28). And He also said, "All that the Father gives me will come to me, and whoever comes to me I will never drive away" (John 6:37).

What does He mean? He simply meant that in this marvelous relationship in which He lived His life on earth, the Father was forever giving Him power over all flesh, over everyone that came—an adequate answer for every need. So He in turn, in meeting that need, gave those individuals back to the Father, having received them as a gift from the Father to Himself.

Do you see that we stand in exactly the same relationship to the Lord Jesus as He stood to His Father? Remember these words, "I tell you the truth, anyone who has faith in me will do what I have been doing. He will do even greater things than these, because I am going to the Father" (John 14:12). All He is saying is that through the life of Jesus Christ in us, He is ready to give to us all power over all flesh. Whatever demand life makes upon us, whatever urgent problem comes bearing down on our lives, He is adequate for it, in order that we might give back to Him the rejoicing and the thanksgiving of our hearts.

Major Ian Thomas has reminded us, "We must have what He is in order to do what He did." That is the secret of vital Christianity. Even in this hour of danger and death, when the cross presses with all its confusing bewilderment upon the Lord Jesus, He prays to the Father and says, "Thank you, Father, the time has come, the time which will mean the greatest blessing the world has ever seen, the time for which I have waited, the time for which I have lived. I know that, in the facing of it, I stand in an adequate relationship which is fully able to meet the demands of that hour."

Intimate Communion

Then there is a third thing with which Jesus introduces this prayer: the unveiling of an unlimited potential. "Now this is eternal life: that they may know you, the only true God, and Jesus Christ, whom you have sent" (John 17:3). What does a Christian mean when he testifies that he has eternal life? What is eternal life? Possibly your answer would be, "It means I will live forever." But is that what eternal life really is? Is it nothing but existence, going on and on forever? Is it life spent on Cloud Nine, eternally strumming a harp? Is it physically walking the golden streets, days and millennia without end?

No, the true definition of eternal life is right in this verse. Jesus says that eternal life is knowing the only true God, and Jesus Christ, whom God has sent. That is eternal life, nothing more, nothing less!

We tend to think eternal life is merely a quantity of time. Jesus says, in effect, "No, eternal life is a quality of relationship!" Eternal life is knowing a Person. When you stop to think about it, that is all which makes life worthwhile, isn't it? What is marriage? Is it three meals a day, bathing the children, watching TV, going to sleep, getting up, going to work in the morning? Is that marriage? No, marriage is knowing another person. That is the essence.

It has been many years now since I sat in the balcony of a church in Montana one fateful Sunday evening. From the Olympian heights of my seat, I saw a beautiful young girl with long, blonde hair singing a solo. She had the most angelic voice I had ever heard. I said to myself in the impetuosity of youth, "There is the girl I'm going to marry." But I felt a terrible sense of frustration, for I was scheduled to leave for Chicago the next morning, where I would be living and working.

After the meeting was dismissed, I met that girl in the doorway of the church, and I asked if I could write to her. I think she was surprised, but she said yes, and I wrote off and on for five or six years. Eventually I moved to Hawaii, but I was still writing to the same girl. And not long after that I persuaded her to come to Hawaii and we were married.

I had been attempting to know her through correspondence all those years, but I really didn't know her very well until we were married. It was then that we began to know each other, and the whole joy of marriage for me is the knowledge of another person. Marriages which do not have that element in them disintegrate and become nothing but a boring, frustrating existence. It is knowing a person that enriches life.

The same is true of the Christian life. Eternal life is the knowledge of an eternal Person, the intimacy of communion and fellowship with the Person of God. "Now this is eternal life: that they may know you, the only true God, and Jesus Christ, whom you have sent."

Enlarging Our Lives

What are the results of knowing God? The result of intimate fellowship (whether between two human beings or between a human being and God) is always the same: life becomes meaningful, rich, and enjoyable. Knowing another person means the end of loneliness. It means a sympathizing heart, someone to whom we may tell our problems and who will share our joys and woes. There is no quality in life like it. And when the person we know, deeply and intimately, is the infinite Person of God, then all of these wonderful benefits are magnified beyond all limits and boundaries. Knowing God is fullness of enjoyment, the richest of experiences, the enlargement of life beyond our ability to imagine.

Have you ever observed that someone who is withdrawn from others, who lives a hermit's life, also lives a very narrow life? His life is bounded by fixed habits on the north and unchangeable attitudes on the south. That is the whole of life for him: a narrow grave with both ends kicked out. But when we come to know other people, and especially when we come to know God, life is enlarged. It takes on breadth as well as length. We discover that the knowledge of God broadens the whole perspective of life until we begin to truly live for the first time.

A number of years ago, I spoke to a group of young adults at a Snow Conference on the Canadian border. After one of the meetings where I spoke about knowing God, a young man came up to me. Though I didn't know it at the time, I later learned that he was a relatively new convert, a young man who had been a test pilot, and who had lived a rather wild life. He said to me, "You know, I like that. You are talking about God differently than anyone I have heard before. You don't make Him sound like He is off there somewhere. Listening to you I could see that God—" He paused and groped for the word to express his meaning. Finally, he said, "God swings!" Of course, these days the expression might be, "God is cool!" or "God is awesome!" But you get the idea.

I understood immediately that there was not the slightest bit of irreverence in what this young man said. He was saying that God is relevant to life—and that knowing God enlarges life. God is not some musty concept reserved for Sunday mornings. God is the ultimate reality, and we are intended to know Him and experience Him on a daily basis. When we do so, life becomes vibrant, exciting, and awesome.

The knowledge of a person adds enjoyment and enlargement to life—but most of all, it adds enrichment. Life must not only have length and breadth, but it must also have depth. As we come to know God through Jesus Christ (for there is no other way to know God), as we give ourselves to the fellowship and obedience of Jesus Christ, we discover that life becomes enriched by Him in all dimensions. For the first time, we begin to experience what human life was intended to be.

A man once told me the story of his life-changing encounter with Jesus Christ. "I was forty-one years old when I discovered Jesus Christ. And I thank God that at forty-one I learned for the first time the true values of life. My father became a Christian only five days before he died, but those last five days were the most wonderful days of his life. I'm just grateful that though my father only understood the real values of life for five days, I have been permitted to know what life is about for a number of years. My life has been so rich since I discovered a personal relationship with the Creator of life."

That is what the knowledge of God brings. Paul says, "So then, no more boasting about men! All things are yours, whether Paul or Apollos or Cephas or the world or life or death or the present or the future—all are yours, and you are of Christ, and Christ is of God" (1 Corinthians 3:21–23). What a magnificent panorama, what tremendous possibilities lie in this simple relationship with Jesus Christ!

Now my question to you is this: Are you praying out of that kind of an understanding, out of that kind of a relationship? Are you seeking to enter into that? Do you really believe that these are the possibilities God is ready to pour into your life? Or are you content, as so many of us are, to plod on week after endless week, doing the same old things with the same old attitudes as the worldlings around us, with nothing visibly different in our lives? That is what our Lord confronts us with in this prayer. In the face of the most tragic hour in human history, there is nothing of nervousness or defeat in the true "Lord's Prayer." Instead, there is simply a resting upon that which has been the characteristic of His life all along—a vibrant, living relationship with God the Father.

Billy Graham tells the true story told him by a pastor he met in Glasgow, Scotland. There was a woman in this pastor's parish who was in financial difficulty and behind in her rent. So the pastor took up a collection at church, a love offering to help this lady catch up her rent. The pastor then went to her home to give her the money. He knocked and knocked and knocked at the door, but there was no answer. Finally, he gave up and went away.

Later, he happened to run into this woman at the market. He told her he had been to her house and explained why. Her eyes widened and she said, "Oh, was that you? I thought it was the landlord and I was afraid to open the door!"

Jesus stands at the door and knocks, ready to make the riches of a relationship with God available to us—riches beyond our imagining. We have only to open the door and receive those riches. The Lord's riches cannot help anyone whose door is shut and barred from within.

So take hold of that relationship which is available to all who believe in Him. Live that relationship, day by day and hour by hour—and your life will be richer, higher, broader, deeper, larger than you could ever imagine!

Our Father, what pathetic beggars we are! We possess such marvelous riches, yet we enjoy so little of them. Lord, strike away the shackles of our unbelief. Stop us from discounting the truth contained in the true Lord's Prayer, which Jesus prayed before going to the cross. Save us from this terrible trap of slipping back into "normal life" as we call it, and being the same old person that we were before.

God, help us to see that in Jesus Christ there is eternal life, light, liberty, abundance. Make us hunger and thirst for the vast, unbounded, enlarged life you offer us.

We pray in the name of Jesus, Amen.

10

Prayer's Possibilities

"I have brought you glory on earth by completing the work you gave me to do. And now, Father, glorify me in your presence with the glory I had with you before the world began.

"I have revealed you to those whom you gave me out of the world. They were yours; you gave them to me and they have obeyed your word. Now they know that everything you have given me comes from you. For I gave them the words you gave me and they accepted them. They knew with certainty that I came from you, and they believed that you sent me."

John 17:4–8

Suppose you knew that your life would come to an end tomorrow. How would you sum up the meaning of your life? How would you explain to someone what you feel were the lasting values of your life?

That is precisely the issue facing Jesus as we continue our study of the true Lord's Prayer in John 17. Earlier, in John 13 (which introduces the Upper Room Discourse), the beloved apostle recorded this story:

> Jesus knew that the Father had put all things under his power, and that he had come from God and was returning to God; so he got up from the meal, took off his outer clothing, and wrapped a towel around his waist. After that, he poured water into a basin and began to wash his disciples' feet, drying them with the towel that was wrapped around him (John 13:3–5).

Immediately after this, Jesus spoke to His disciples in the amazing words we call the Upper Room Discourse. When He turns to prayer at the close of this discourse, our Lord reviews His life to the Father—a review of thirty-three years of ministry on earth: those silent years in Nazareth and those action-packed years in His public ministry when He went up and down the hills of Judea and Galilee, preaching and healing and ministering to all the multitudes that followed Him.

As we read these words, we are privileged to listen in while He appraises His own life. He is gathering all these thirty-three years into three tremendous statements, which constitute His own evaluation of the greatest life ever lived. The first thing He points out to the Father is that He accomplished a work which glorifies:

"I have brought you glory on earth by completing the work you gave me to do. And now, Father, glorify me in your presence with the glory I had with you before the world began" (John 17:4–5).

Although this prayer was prayed before the cross, in its scope it includes the cross—and even reaches beyond the cross. Our Lord knew where He was going, what He would be doing in the next few hours, and what would be accomplished. In view of this, He says that He has completed the work that the Father gave Him to do.

Before the World Was Made

The work that the Father gave Jesus to do included more than the cross. It encompassed His ministry of healing and mercy, and as I have suggested, even those thirty silent years back in Nazareth, of which we know so little. They were all part of His life, the work His Father had given Him to do. The key to the meaning of this is found in verse 5: "And now, Father, glorify me in your presence"— where Jesus was soon going—"with the glory I had with you before the world began."

No other human lips could utter those words. None of us can look back to a time when we were with the Father before the world was made—only Jesus could. And in saying this, He is asking to be restored to the glory that is properly His. If there is any verse in the Bible which unmistakably reflects the deity of Jesus Christ, it is this verse. For here He is asking for the glory which was the Father's glory as well.

Isaiah reminds us that God does not share His glory with anyone less than Himself. "I am the LORD; that is my name!" says God in Isaiah 42:8. "I will not give my glory to another or my praise to idols." But here is One who shared the Father's glory before the world was made and who recognizes that it was properly His.

It would be interesting to dwell upon that glory and consider what it was and how He could recall it as a man walking here on the earth, but this is not the point our Lord is making. He brings this up to indicate the character of His work while He was here.

Jesus is suggesting that His work was characterized by a continual self-emptying—a laying aside of glory. Now that He has reached the end He is ready to resume the glory which was properly His, but He is thinking back over thirty-three years of His life and recognizing that all during that time He had voluntarily surrendered His right to be worshiped, His right to the glory that belonged to God.

This brings to mind Paul's words about Jesus, "Who, being in very nature God, did not consider equality with God something to be grasped, but made himself nothing, taking the very nature of a servant, being made in human likeness" (Philippians 2:6–7). Self-emptying—that is what glorifies God.

We are so confused about this. We think that God is interested in our activity, that our religious efforts will please Him, no matter what our motives or attitude. That is why we often drag ourselves out to church, week after week, when we actually have little interest in attending church, because we think that going to church is what God wants. Or we donate to some missionary cause because we think this is what God is after. How little we understand God!

It is not activity He desires. It was not merely that which Jesus did which glorified the Father. It was not His ministry of mercy and good works. Others have done similar works. But it was the fact that, throughout His life, He had a heart that was ready to obey, an ear that was ready to hear, a will that was ready to be subject to the Father. It was His willingness to be always available, to be forever giving of Himself, that glorified God.

Think back on the incident at the baptism of Jesus by John when the heavens opened and the voice of the Father came in thunderous tones: "This is my Son, whom I love; with him I am well pleased" (Matthew 3:17). He had not done anything yet—that was only the beginning of His ministry—but for thirty years in obscurity He had been delighting the heart of the Father. During those years, as in all His ministry, He manifested a heart that was ready to obey. That is what glorifies God.

The Cost of Rebellion

Many books have been written about the so-called "cost of discipleship." They declare in one way or another that in order to have power with God we must pay a high price. In various ways they state that becoming a victorious Christian, an effective Christian, requires a difficult and demanding discipline.

I am not impressed with this type of literature because it sets forth a totally negative approach. It puts the cart before the horse. I don't mean that such an approach is not true, for obedience to God does mean saying no to a lot of other things. You cannot say yes to the Spirit of God without, at the same time, saying no to many other things—this is simply inherent in the process of decision. So I'm not saying that living for the glory of God doesn't cost us certain fancied pleasures and relationships which perhaps we want to hold on to. But I think we would do well to focus less on the cost of discipleship and focus more on the cost of disobedience—because it is disobedience that truly exacts a punishing cost from our lives.

You know the kind of cost I'm talking about. What a tremendous toll our disobedience and our unwillingness to give of ourselves takes in our lives. Payment is exacted in terms of frustrated, restless spirits, and in shameful, degrading acts that we hope nobody discovers—skeletons that rattle around in the closet of our conscience for years. Or our lives are depleted through emotional states of bitterness, resentment, guilt, and anxiety that keep us in a nervous frenzy all the time.

But the greatest toll, in some ways, is that of self-righteousness. In order to cover up our disobedience, we often rig a façade of smug religiosity which we call "Christianity." This is a stench in the nostrils of the world and an offense to God.

Where do these attitudes and actions come from? Are they not the terrible price we pay for a rebellious spirit, for an unwillingness to yield ourselves to the Lordship of Christ? We are not our own, we say, but we still cling to the right to run our own lives and make our own decisions, to choose our own pleasures, go where we will, and do what we want. And then we cover it over with pious religiosity! We say we want to do God's will, as long as it is what we want to do. At the center of our lives, self is still king—and that is the problem. Our own glory is in view. We still want what we want and we are not willing, as Jesus was, to walk in glad obedience even though that is what glorifies the Father.

Let us not talk about living to the glory of God while our own lives are still filled with so much self-centeredness and selfishness. Do you realize that every truly great Christian who ever lived has found that the glory of an obedient life far outweighs the piddling cost of giving up a few selfish desires for Christ's sake? Don't talk about the cost of discipleship; it is the cost of rebellion that we ought to be concerned about.

C. T. Studd, who gave away his fortune and went out into the heart of Africa, said, "If Jesus Christ be God and died for me, then there is no sacrifice too great for me to make for Him." Missionary David Livingstone said, "I have resolved not to count anything I own of any value, save as it relates to the advance of the Kingdom of God." Was this sacrifice? They would not call it that. Those who have seen the glory of God in an obedient heart never speak of sacrifice. They never talk about what they have given up, because what they have gotten is of such tremendous, surpassing value. Paul could say, "But whatever was to my profit I now consider loss for the sake of Christ" (Philippians 3:7). Nothing could compare with what Christ could give to him.

A few years ago, on a hillside in Korea, a man was buried who for many years lived as a simple farmer in Oregon. On a trip to that Asian land he saw the needs of the desolate, destitute orphans of Korea—thousands of children fathered by American soldiers who served in Korea, then went home, leaving these children behind. This man saw the orphaned children of Korea as every other tourist who goes to Korea sees them—out in the streets, penniless, begging, with no one to care for them.

But unlike the other tourists, he did not go on to some other country and forget what he saw. He came home and began to line up homes in America for Korean orphans. He had suffered a heart attack already, and had been forewarned by his doctor not to overexert himself, but he forgot that—he forgot himself and gave of himself without reservation.

The week of his death, the story of this man's work appeared in every English language newspaper in the world, for here was a man who had lost himself so that he might glorify God. His name was Harry Holt.

Now as Jesus is talking to the Father, He puts His finger right on the thing that glorifies God, a life of self-giving love. What are we giving ourselves to? Who are we helping?

The Power That Works

Next, Jesus reveals the second thing that marks His life: "I have revealed you to those whom you gave me out of the world. They were yours; you gave them to me and they have obeyed your word" (John 17:6). That is an amazing statement, "They have obeyed your word." He says, "I have manifested a name that empowers men to keep God's word." There is a relationship between these two. What was the result in the disciples' lives when the name of God became manifest? They kept God's word.

We often fail to realize that ignorance of right and wrong is seldom the problem. It is not that we do not know what God wants us to do. The truth is, we do not want to do it! In fact, in some way strange to us, we cannot do it; our wills are paralyzed. We may want to, but we cannot.

I will never forget, years ago, a young man with agony in his eyes laying hold of my arm and saying, "What do you do when you know something is wrong and you don't want to do it—but even while you are promising that you won't do it, you know that you are going to do it again? What do you do then?" The only answer I have found to that question is to understand and act on what God is willing to be to us. In other words, we need to understand the character of God, to lay hold of His name—that is the true power of human life and the only power that works.

A name stands for the total character and resources of an individual. My name is all that I am, your name is all that you are. Whatever you are, that is what your name means to others. When my wife took my name in marriage, she literally took me for all I had. It wasn't much! As a matter of fact, we had to cash her bonds to get home from the honeymoon. But whenever I sign my name, "Ray C. Stedman," the whole Stedman fortune, all thirty-five dollars of it, is laid on the line.

Now the work of Jesus Christ during those thirty-three years of His life was to unveil to us the total resources of the Father, to manifest His name, so that we might discover what a tremendous, unending resource we have in God. We can never get to the bottom of the barrel—but we fail to realize how inexhaustibly great His resources are. Failure to realize the resources of God is the source of our weakness.

I continually see Christians struggling, trying to act by faith, and yet all the time sabotaging their efforts by a flat refusal to believe that God is what He says He is. It is amazing to me how easily we believe the satanic lies about God. We do not believe that God is what He says He is. We believe, essentially, that God is utterly faithless and that He will not do what He says He will do.

When I talk with people and they tell me their troubles, I try to give them counsel from God's Word. No matter what I suggest, however, many tell me in one way or another that they've tried it without success. I wish I had a nickel for every time I've heard the phrase, "I've tried that, but . . ." They say they have done everything required, but God does not act, and they have come to believe that He is capricious and unreliable. He will do things for someone else, but He won't do it for them. When we believe that kind of lie, we undermine every effort God makes to give us the victory in life.

"God is faithful." How many times does the Scripture say that? "And God is faithful; he will not let you be tempted beyond what you can bear. But when you are tempted, he will also provide a way out so that you can stand up under it" (1 Corinthians 10:13). "God, who has called you into fellowship with his Son Jesus Christ our Lord, is faithful" (1 Corinthians 1:9).

The whole work of Jesus Christ is to show us the faithfulness of God. What a glory is manifested in His life as we see how He rested on God's faithfulness. He was not anxious, He was not troubled, He was not disturbed when the clouds of oppression and persecution began to hang heavy over Him, for He rested on the faithful name of God. "The name of the LORD is a strong tower; the righteous run to it and are safe" (Proverbs 18:10). Have you discovered the faithfulness of God?

To Awaken Faith

There is yet a third thing Jesus said characterized His life: "For I gave them the words you gave me and they accepted them. They knew with certainty that I came from you, and they believed that you sent me" (John 17:8). What made these Jewish disciples, who were mortally afraid of idolatry, believe that this man with whom they had lived, eaten, and slept, with whom they had walked the roads of Galilee and Judea, whom they had seen in all the weakness of His human life—what made them believe that Jesus was incarnate God, sent of the Father?

John could write: "In the beginning was the Word, and the Word was with God, and the Word was God" (John 1:1). How did he learn that? Was it Jesus' miracles that convinced him? No, His miracles never convinced anyone of His deity. They convinced them of His Messiahship; that is what they were designed to do. Was it the power that He exercised over people? No, there have been many evil people who have exercised tremendous power over the minds and hearts of others. It wasn't that. So what was it?

His words! The words of Jesus searched their hearts, opened their eyes, dispelled their doubts, and set their lives afire. They knew that when they took these words seriously, things happened to them that only God could do. Gradually, through the course of three and one-half years, as they listened to those compelling, magnetic words, there was born in their hearts the faith that here was One who came from God.

The words of Jesus still have that power today. Are you troubled by doubts as to your Christian faith? In these days when there is so great an attack against the foundations of faith, it wouldn't be surprising if you were. If you are troubled with doubts, may I suggest something? Start reading the words of Jesus and take them seriously. Don't just read them, take them as a revelation of basic underlying truth. Take them seriously. You won't read far before discovering so much understanding of life and experience that you cannot help but believe that these words are indeed the words of God.

What pitiful groping exists among Christians today. I am troubled by the way young theologians, new graduates of seminaries, frankly admit that they are better acquainted with the writings of Tillich, Barth, and Bultmann than they are with the writings of Moses and Paul and the words of Jesus Christ. No wonder they have weak foundations for their faith! Nothing convinces like the matchless Word of God.

Here are the three things that Jesus came to do. He said, "I came to give myself in a self-emptying ministry; I came to manifest an all-empowering Name by which anything that needs to be done may be done; and I came to speak compelling words that would awaken faith in men's hearts and cause them to believe." John said at the beginning of this discourse that Jesus knew the Father had given all things into His hands. He knew that He had come from God, and He knew that He was going to God. In between lay those thirty-three years whose impact the world can never escape, which He is gathering up in these three brief phrases: a work accomplished, a name manifested, and words uttered to awaken faith. Jesus came from God and He went to God. That is what the authentic Christian life is all about.

Now tell me, where did you get your Christian life? Did you have it when you were born into this world? Of course not, you got it when you believed in Jesus Christ. It came from God. It was with the Father before you received it because it was in Jesus Christ. This life is in His Son. "He who has the Son has life; he who does not have the Son of God does not have life" (1 John 5:12).

What happens to your life when you get through with it here on earth? Where does it go? Every Christian believes it goes to the Father. "I desire to depart and be with Christ, which is better by far," says Paul (Philippians 1:23). So these words are true of you, as well. It came from God, it goes to God.

And what is in between? A life that glorifies the Father, manifesting before the world the Name that empowers people; a life that speaks the words that grip human hearts and calls human beings to a realization of their own need and an understanding of truth and reality.

In John 17, Jesus offers a prayer that includes all of us, and the astonishing thing is that there is not a word that you and I cannot pray as well. May God lead us to lay hold of the transforming, dynamic Christian life that Jesus Himself manifested.

Father, these words of the Lord Jesus search us, they reveal to us things that we have never known before—truths so towering and awesome that we can scarcely believe them! But Lord, help us to remember where these truths come from. Help us to trust that, because they come from you, they are true and we can stand on them with boldness and confidence.

Keep us from being ineffective, ordinary Christians. Challenge us to be true followers of you, ready to fling our lives away for Jesus Christ, ready to be utterly careless of what happens to us in order that He may be glorified.

We pray in His name, Amen.

11

Christal Prays for You

"I pray for them. I am not praying for the world, but for those you have given me, for they are yours. All I have is yours, and all you have is mine. And glory has come to me through them. I will remain in the world no longer, but they are still in the world, and I am coming to you. Holy Father, protect them by the power of your name—the name you gave me—so that they may be one as we are one. While I was with them, I protected them and kept them safe by that name you gave me. None has been lost except the one doomed to destruction so that Scripture would be fulfilled.

"I am coming to you now, but I say these things while I am still in the world, so that they may have the full measure of my joy within them. I have given them your word and the world has hated them, for they are not of the world any more than I am of the world. My prayer is not that you take them out of the world but that you protect them from the evil one. They are not of the world, even as I am not of it. Sanctify them by the truth; your word is truth. As you sent me into the world, I have sent them into the world. For them I sanctify myself, that they too may be truly sanctified."

John 17:9–19

As Jesus prepared to leave His disciples and move on to the cross, they felt frightened, helpless, and unable to understand what was taking place. They could not see that our Lord was merely introducing a higher and better relationship to them. Don't we often feel this way? God leads us to a place of change and we are frightened by it. We wonder if we are not losing everything we once held dear. We scarcely realize that God is only leading us to a higher, newer, and greater relationship. Like these disciples we are frightened and fearful.

As we come to our study of these words of Jesus in John 17:9–19, my concern is how to convey something of the gripping reality of the requests of Jesus—something of the intense practicality of what Jesus is saying. I am so afraid that we will listen to these words as we would to beautiful poetry or a moving drama, and, entranced by their familiarity and beauty, fail to realize that Jesus is actually praying here for us, for you and me, for the practical needs of our daily lives.

This prayer ought to hit us in the face like a bucket of ice water. Or, perhaps, like a hand that grabs us and rescues us as we are going down for the third time. These words ought both to sober us and to comfort us. They are not soft, beautiful words, prayed in a great cathedral, but earthy, gutsy words, uttered on a battlefield in which our Lord is coming to grips with evil as it really is. So these words ought to resonate within us as we recognize the truth of our own daily reality in them.

Kept and Preserved

Dr. Jean Henri d'Aubigne (1794–1872) was a Swiss historian of the Reformation. During a visit to Scotland, he stayed with the Scottish preacher Thomas Chalmers. One morning, Dr. Chalmers served his Swiss houseguest a breakfast of kippered herring—something Dr. d'Aubigne had never tasted before. Dr. d'Aubigne asked his Scottish host what the word *kippered* meant.

"Oh," replied Dr. Chalmers, "*kippered* means 'kept' or 'preserved.' "

"Ah," said Dr. d'Aubigne, nodding his understanding.

The two men spent the day together, discussing the Scottish Reformation. At the end of the day, they prayed together, and Dr. d'Aubigne prayed, "Oh, Father, I pray that Dr. Chalmers might be kept, preserved, and kippered by your grace."

In John 17:11, Jesus does not pray that we would be "kippered," but He does pray that we would be kept and preserved: "I will remain in the world no longer, but they are still in the world, and I am coming to you. Holy Father, protect them by the power of your name—the name you gave me—so that they may be one as we are one." Later in this prayer, He adds, "My prayer is not that you take them out of the world but that you protect them from the evil one" (John 17:15).

This is the theme of His prayer for His disciples, both then and now: that all who follow Him might be kept and preserved. Why? There are so many things that I would pray for if I were in His place (if any mere man could be in His place!). They are the usual things we pray for one another: "Use them," "strengthen them," "teach them," or "guide them." But now that Jesus is leaving His disciples, He wants to put into one brief phrase His entire heart's desire for them. So He sums it up in those two little words, "Keep them!"

The more I reflected on this prayer of Jesus, the more I realized that this is very much how I pray when I am about to leave my family or when I am away from them. When I am with my loved ones, I can pray more specifically for them, but when I am away, I am continually praying, "Lord, keep them, keep them." All of this simply points up the fact which is highlighted for us here in this prayer of Jesus: relationship is supreme. Whom we are with is far more important than what we do. Whom you fellowship with determines what you are, so Jesus' prayer is that His followers' relationship with the Father remain intact, for from that relationship everything else He desires will come.

Worldliness Unmasked

So He prays, "Keep them." As He prays, our Lord has in view the peril in the world. He says,

> "I have given them your word and the world has hated them, for they are not of the world any more than I am of the world. My prayer is not that you take them out of the world but that you protect them from the evil one" (John 17:14–15).

Our Lord saw very clearly into the nature of life as it is the nature of reality. He realized that Christians face a hostile world, behind which there is a sinister being of incredible subtlety whom we call the devil. We do not see the devil, the evil one—but it would be helpful if we could! He would be much more easily dealt with if he were visible, but unfortunately he is not. He keeps himself behind the scenes and thus has created the myth that he does not even exist.

But in the eyes of Jesus, who saw things as they really were, the devil was a very real being. And while, as human beings, we cannot see the devil, we are able to see his fortress, which Jesus calls "the world." Christians have struggled with this problem of the world and have wondered what it means all through the twenty centuries of this Christian age. There are some who have made the mistake of thinking it is the world of nature, and that Christians ought not to have anything to do with the enjoyment of natural beauty—the glories of the mountains and the sea, the whole world of natural life. This is certainly not true. Others have wondered if it means the world of natural relationships, our family life, friends, home, the relationships between mothers and fathers and children. No, this is not "the world" of which our Lord warns.

The term "world," as it is used here, means preeminently the basic assumptions which men and women make who live without God. In other words, Jesus is talking about a secular philosophy of life.

Some time ago I received an invitation to subscribe to a magazine that was, I felt, extremely worldly. It was a new publication and, as I read the prospectus, it seemed to me that this magazine would espouse a consistent line of worldly philosophy. I subscribed to it for that reason, expecting to receive a window on our declining culture—and probably a few sermon illustrations as well. The magazine did not disappoint me! In its pages, the worldly philosophy of this dying age was boldly proclaimed. Here was worldliness unmasked!

I read through two issues and jotted down a few statements to illustrate what I mean. From one article these words are taken:

It is the moralists who are responsible for our present level of sex crime and the state of affairs revealed in the Kinsey Report. The world is sick with morality.

The problems of poverty and racial injustice and political corruption and everything else, are all branches of a single evil tree, and that tree is Authority. Obedience to authority is the one single principle that explains every evil in human history.

The Freudian concepts of sex-motivation can adequately explain all human phenomena.

Organized religion is a tough old rooster which has traditionally been first in the American pecking-order. The press can peck the government, the government can peck industry, industry can peck labor, and labor can peck all three of them back, but nobody can peck the rooster and the rooster can always peck anyone else at any time with impunity.

The problem, they say, is the church.

I gathered these statements to document what Jesus says: The world hates His disciples because they are not of the world. The world in which we live is dominated by a satanic philosophy which is diametrically opposed to all that God stands for. We make a serious mistake when we forget that fact and try to settle down in this world and become comfortable in it as though this were the climate in which we ought to feel at home.

Perhaps the most effective propaganda in the world is the satanic lie that the purpose of life is to experience an endless series of emotional highs—from the sensual thrill of sexual promiscuity to the artificial highs of drugs and alcohol to the excitement of living on the edge and going to extremes. Our entertainment and advertising media shout to us that life is a series of electrifying experiences—and those who are not spending their time bed-hopping or sky-boarding or hang-gliding are letting life pass them by. Certainly, many of our younger generation are buying into this satanic lie.

The fact is, life was never intended to be all moonlight and roses, swashbuckling adventure, or breath-taking journeys to faraway places. It is a bitter irony of our day, perhaps more than in any other age, that we have more diversions, more gadgets, more satellite-TV channels, more websites to explore on the Internet, more computer and video games, more leisure-time diversions, and more pornography, more phone sex and computer sex, more drugs, more parties, and on and on and on—yet people have never been more anxious, nervous, neurotic, depressed, guilt-ridden, fearful, insecure, restless, bored, depressed, or suicidal than they are today. When we have surrounded ourselves with all that our dreams have envisaged, we find our lives are still empty and without meaning. The promise of the good life is all a mirage.

The Christian answer to this satanic lie of the world is found in John 17:13: "I am coming to you now, but I say these things while I am still in the world, so that they may have the full measure of my joy within them." That is where joy lies. That is where we can find fulfillment, meaning, purpose, and blessing—not in pursuing the will-o'-the-wisp of illicit sex or adrenaline-rush adventures, and not in acquiring more and more material things. True satisfaction only comes to those who are committed to Jesus Christ, who are in a relationship with Him. Here is a way of living filled with an unexplainable joy that simply cannot be compared with anything else.

A few years ago I heard a man say, "I have had so much fun in my life that I can hardly describe it. Life, to me, has been a continually exciting thing." Who was that? Was it someone who has given himself to the search for adventure? Was it Hugh Hefner, the Playboy mogul who has given his life to the quest for hedonism and the spread of immorality? Was it a rich entrepreneur such as Donald Trump, Bill Gates, or Ted Turner? Was it a famous actor, such as Tom Cruise or Shirley MacLaine? No, the man who said those words was Dr. Frank Laubach, who, as a Christian, lost himself in the cause of teaching people all over the world to read so they would be able to read the words of life and truth in the Scripture.

A young man once told me, "I am a radio physicist. I work on the frontiers of the exciting world of science, exploring the universe. But I must say that this exciting realm of science in which I work seems a dull business compared to the excitement that comes from discovering and exploring a relationship with Jesus Christ."

A Supernatural Task

Where do we find the power to live the Christian life in the midst of a hostile, alluring, antichristian world? Bombarded on all sides by satanic lies and seductive pleasures and thrills, how do we live out God's truth? The only possible answer is that we must rely on the very same power that our Lord relies on in John 17. He identifies that power in two places (which I have italicized below) in this prayer:

> "I will remain in the world no longer, but they are still in the world, and I am coming to you. Holy Father, protect them *by the power of your name*—the name you gave

me—so that they may be one as we are one. While I was
with them, I protected them and kept them safe *by that
name you gave me.* None has been lost except the one
doomed to destruction so that Scripture would be fulfilled" (John 17:11–12, emphasis added).

As we have already seen, the name of God stands for
all the authority and resources of God. Jesus says here that
keeping a believer from the allurements and deceit of the
world is a supernatural task. No man is smart enough to do
it on his own—only the power of the name and the authority of God can keep us.

The fact that we can trust the power of God to keep
us and preserve us is reflected throughout the Epistles of
the New Testament. Paul said, "I know whom I have
believed, and am convinced that he is able to guard what I
have entrusted to him for that day" (2 Timothy 1:12).
Peter speaks of those "who through faith are shielded by
God's power until the coming of the salvation that is
ready to be revealed in the last time" (1 Peter 1:5). And
almost the last promise of Scripture is that word of Jude's,
"To him who is able to keep you from falling and to present you before his glorious presence without fault and
with great joy" (Jude 24). Nothing else will suffice to save
and keep us—only the power of God.

Just as in the saying that "the exception proves the
rule," Jesus proves God's preserving power by highlighting
the one apparent exception, Judas Iscariot. "While I was
with them, I protected them and kept them safe by that
name you gave me. None has been lost except the one
doomed to destruction so that Scripture would be fulfilled"
(John 17:12). What a sobering, frightening possibility is
revealed in Judas. Here is a man who was one of the disci-

ples, personally called and taught by Jesus, included in the intimate, inner circle of the twelve, a highly religious man, a man who was dedicated to the cause of God as he saw it. He was an earnest man of strong convictions—even though not above a little pilfering from the bag now and then.

There was one thing wrong with Judas: He thought he could keep himself by his own efforts. He thought he could follow Christ in his own strength and use Christ for his own ends. Judas had never made that inner surrender of the heart by which he recognized his utter weakness and cast himself on Christ. He had never come to the place of saying, as we sing in that old hymn, "Nothing in my hand I bring, simply to thy cross I cling." He had never come to Christ, desperately aware of his own weakness, as the other disciples had.

Despite all his faults and instability, Peter had cast himself upon the Lord. He had surrendered completely to Christ. "Lord," Peter said to Him in John 6:68, "to whom shall we go? You have the words of eternal life."

Jesus calls Judas "the one doomed to destruction," or (in the King James Version) "the son of perdition." How did this happen to Judas? I don't believe he became "the son of perdition" when he betrayed Jesus. I believe the betrayal was simply the result of the fact that he had been "the son of perdition" all along. He had never been anything else.

He never was in the Father's keeping power, so the Father could not keep him. But those who have learned not to trust themselves, who have, as Paul says, "no confidence in the flesh," are kept by the Father's name—and Jesus says that nothing, nothing, NOTHING can separate them from the love of the Father. "My Father, who has given them to me, is greater than all; no one can snatch them out of my Father's hand" (John 10:29).

Do We Follow Feelings—Or God's Truth?

In verses 17 through 19, Jesus delves into a subject that we often hear about in the church, but which, I suspect, many Christians understand very little—the subject of sanctification:

> "Sanctify them by the truth; your word is truth. As you sent me into the world, I have sent them into the world. For them I sanctify myself, that they too may be truly sanctified."

That troublesome word *sanctify* or *sanctification* appears three times in these three verses. What does Jesus mean? I do not know of any other word in Scripture that is more misunderstood. The word *sanctify* simply means "to put to the proper use." I am sanctifying a microphone when I use it to amplify my voice. I am sanctifying the pulpit when I preach. I am sanctifying the printed page when I write a book. You sanctify your living room recliner when you ease back in it and read a good book. When you put something to its proper use, you sanctify it.

So when Jesus says to the Father, "Sanctify them," He means, "Father, by your power, enable these men and women to accomplish the purpose that you have in mind for them. Put them to their proper use. Let them find the reason they were born. Bring them to the place where they discover your program for them." How? "By the truth," says Jesus, "your word is truth."

In the vast, eternal program of God, what is our part? What must we do to become a part of His program, so that He can sanctify us and put us to our proper use? Why, our part is simply to believe the truth! You may be thinking, "Is that all? That's what preachers always say—'Believe the truth, believe the truth!' "

And while it's true that preachers do say that all the time, it is also true that believing the truth is one of the most difficult things the human heart attempts to do. Why? Because our feelings keep getting in the way! The brutal fact is that we much prefer to believe our feelings than the Word. That is where our problem lies. More than once, Christians have said to me, "I simply cannot take it any longer, I give up. Scripture doesn't seem to work for me. I try to fulfill the promises, I try to rely on the Lord, I try to appropriate Christ, I try to do all these things, but it doesn't work for me. It may work for you, but it doesn't work for me. I can't take the pressures that come, I can't take the testings that I am subjected to."

Whenever people say that to me, I remind them of what Paul says, "No temptation has seized you except what is common to man. And God is faithful; he will not let you be tempted beyond what you can bear. But when you are tempted, he will also provide a way out so that you can stand up under it" (1 Corinthians 10:13). And then I add my own commentary: "So don't get discouraged. You are not going through anything that others have not gone through."

Almost invariably, the reaction is, "That can't be! Nobody else has gone through what I am going through! I simply can't believe that what I'm going through is a common experience. You don't understand what I am going through! Nobody understands! No one!" Now, that is nothing more than disguised unbelief—a refusal to accept what God says is true. And that is our fundamental problem, isn't it? We say we believe, but we do not believe, because when it comes down to the actual, real-life application of God's truth, we really mean, "God can't be trusted, my feelings are what is true! I operate on my feelings, not on what God tells me." And so we make God out to be a liar, while enshrining our feelings as our god.

Suppose you went to a friend and asked, "How do you go about traveling by airliner? I've never flown before, and I don't even know how to buy a ticket. Tell me how it's done."

Your friend replies, "Well, it's simple. Just call the airline that goes to the destination you desire and make a reservation. Then you buy a ticket and you present that ticket at the proper time at the airport and you will be admitted to the plane. Then you get aboard the plane, sit down in your seat, and fasten your seatbelt—the plane does all the rest!"

You're still a little hesitant. "But," you say, "I'm not sure I understand all the steps. Could you write it down for me?"

So your friend nods, takes a piece of paper, and writes, "Call airline, make reservation, buy ticket, go to airport, present ticket at the proper time, get on plane, that's all."

A few days later, you go back to your friend and say, "Well, I tried it, but it doesn't work. I made the reservation, bought the ticket, went down to the airport, and you know what they told me? They said the plane left two hours ago! This air travel thing just doesn't work! From now on, I'm going to just take the bus."

"Wait a minute," your friend says. "Remember, I said in the instructions, 'present ticket at the proper time.' Did you do that?"

"Oh," you respond, "I read that, but I didn't think it was all that important. After all, one time is as good as another. I went when I was ready."

"Well," says your friend, "there's your trouble. If you are going to act on any of the instructions, you must act on all of them. You cannot leave out any part. If you fail in one part, it cancels out the whole program. You did not go at the proper time, so it didn't work for you."

Now, that's a simple analogy, but I think it's an apt parallel to what frequently goes on in our Christian experience. We must believe that God has told us the truth. There is no value in Christian faith at all if we do not believe that. If the Bible is nothing more than another voice among the thousands that blare at us all week long, giving advice and counsel, then it is utterly worthless. But here is the revelation of truth, of things as they are, regardless of how we feel.

We shall never make any progress in our spiritual lives until we come to grips with the fact that what God says is true. As Paul says, "Let God be true, and every man a liar" (Romans 3:4). When we start believing what He says and act upon it, we discover that all that He says is gloriously confirmed.

It is true that God protects us and keeps us even when our faith fails; thank God for that. He is the Author and the Finisher of faith, and our faith rests upon the foundation of His faithfulness. But it is also true that we will never go any farther than our faith takes us. God may awaken faith anew in us, but we can never make any progress, we can never lay hold of any truth, we can never appropriate any blessing that does not come through the door of a simple trust in the truth of God.

So Jesus prays, in effect, "Sanctify them, put them to the proper use, let them discover what life is all about, by the truth. Father, your word is truth. It is the basis I have built my life and ministry on. As you have sent me into the world to live by continually relying on your power, I now send them into the world to live on exactly the same basis.

I have given them an example. I have sanctified myself before their eyes, living by reliance upon your truth rather than my own senses and feelings. Now sanctify them and put them to the proper use by empowering them to live the same way, consecrated by your truth."

That is our Lord's prayer for us. That is our Lord's example to us. That is God's Word to us, and His Word is truth. May we live by that example, trusting in that truth.

Father, we pray that the words of Jesus we have just studied may not be simply words of beauty. May they instead be a practical blueprint for our daily lives, instructing us in how to build a life that is sanctified, holy, blessed, empowered, and victorious.

Lord, teach us to turn a deaf ear to the seductive voices of this dying age. Open our ears to hear your voice of truth. Open our eyes to see the vision of reality you have set before us. Sanctify us by your Word, for your Word is truth. As we step out in faith, trusting in your truth and not in our own changeable feelings and fallible senses, we thank you, Father, because you are leading us into the assurance of your incredible, unexplainable joy.

For that, we give thanks in Christ's name, Amen.

12

The Prayer for Unity

"My prayer is not for them alone. I pray also for those who will believe in me through their message, that all of them may be one, Father, just as you are in me and I am in you. May they also be in us so that the world may believe that you have sent me. I have given them the glory that you gave me, that they may be one as we are one: I in them and you in me. May they be brought to complete unity to let the world know that you sent me and have loved them even as you have loved me.

"Father, I want those you have given me to be with me where I am, and to see my glory, the glory you have given me because you loved me before the creation of the world.

Righteous Father, though the world does not know you, I know you, and they know that you have sent me. I have made you known to them, and will continue to make you known in order that the love you have for me may be in them and that I myself may be in them."

John 17:20–26

The first General Assembly of the newly founded United Nations was held in temporary headquarters at Lake Success, New York, in 1946. It was a historic occasion—a world summit, a gathering of delegates from most of the nations of the world, in search of a lasting peace. As the first day of the first U. N. General Assembly drew to a close, the president of the General Assembly, Belgian statesman Paul Henri Spaak, addressed the delegates with these words: "Our agenda is now exhausted. The secretary general is exhausted. All of you are exhausted. I find it comforting that, beginning with our very first day, we find ourselves in such complete unanimity."

In the last six verses of "The True Lord's Prayer," our Lord's prayer for us in John 17, we catch a fascinating glimpse of an even more elevated summit meeting, a more exalted agenda, a more glorious unanimity than has ever prevailed in any earthly summit. Here we see a great planning session between the Father, Son, and Holy Spirit—and, like eaves-droppers at the door, we are privileged to listen in on the God's grand plan for history.

The high-level discussion at this divine summit does not focus on a single country or continent of the world, but it takes in the entire world. The purpose of the summit is not to plan a campaign of a few years or a decade or two. Rather, it encompasses the entire age in which we live, from the first coming of Christ to the second coming. It does not involve a few local churches or a denomination or two in some kind of united campaign. Instead, it gathers together the entire global, historic body of Christ—every Christian who has ever lived or ever will live in all time. In a real sense, these verses are the key to history, the blueprint of God's program for this age. From another viewpoint, this is the plan of a military campaign which is designed to recapture this rebellious planet for God.

Target: The World

A number of years ago a British army major taught me the three essentials of military planning: objective, strategy, and tactics. He explained to me the difference between these three essentials: The *objective* is the goal, the hilltop you wish to take or the city that needs to be captured; the *strategy* is the general procedure, the overall plan by which it is proposed to take the objective; the *tactics* are the specific maneuvers by which the strategy is carried out. Every successful military campaign must include all three of these.

In this prayer of Jesus, which was not prayed in a quiet sanctuary but on a battlefield, you have all three ingredients of a military campaign. You can see these three ingredients in these six verses by looking closely. Twice in this section, Jesus states the great objective which was constantly before Him as He lived His life on earth. Now that He is leaving, He is committing that objective to His disciples.

Twice He outlines specifically the objective God intends to accomplish. In the latter part of John 17:21, He says, "so that the world may believe that you have sent me." And again, in the latter part of verse 23, He says, "to let the world know that you sent me." There is the great objective. God's whole redemptive plan is aimed at one target: the world. "For God so loved the world that he gave his one and only Son, that whoever believes in him shall not perish but have eternal life" (John 3:16).

It is so easy for Christians to forget this. Forgetting that we were once part of this world, we become so absorbed in His work in us as believers that we ignore the fact that He is still aiming beyond us. We seem to feel that God's program stops with us, that His entire purpose in coming into the world and leaving by the cross and the resurrection is to get us to heaven.

We must understand, however, that our purpose here as Christians is not to improve the world. Sometimes we become so concerned about needed social and political changes that we give the impression that the church exists in order to make the world a better place in which to live. But that misses the point of God's plan entirely! The whole picture given by Scripture is that no matter what the church does, as God's instrument in the world, the ultimate end of the world will be anarchy and chaos. It will end exactly as Jesus Christ described it, despite the best efforts of the church, and it was never intended otherwise. No, the church is not here to improve the world. Much less is the church here to save the world. We are here for one grand purpose, which Jesus states in this prayer to the Father: "So that the world may believe that you have sent me."

An Opportunity to Choose

Jesus left the church in the world so that the worldlings may become convinced that:

- Jesus Christ is the authentic voice of God.
- His is the authoritative word concerning what God intends to do in human affairs.
- He is the key to world history and reality.
- He is the revelation of the invisible God and the only way from man to God.

When the worldlings become convinced of these truths, the rest is up to them. Our task, as believers in Jesus

Christ, is not to save the world; our job is to bring it to an awareness of Him so that worldlings will do one of two things: Either accept Him and be saved, or reject Him and continue in the lost condition in which the whole world exists.

While attending a missionary conference in Pasadena, California, several years ago, I attended a session in which a panel of missionaries and mission leaders were being questioned. One of the questions asked was, "What is the definition of world evangelism?" Several answers were given, but the one which impressed me most was: "World evangelism is the attempt to give every person an opportunity to make an intelligent choice of whether to receive or reject Jesus Christ." Excellent definition! That is exactly what world evangelism is!

So, for the sake of a confused and sinful world which is facing enormously complex problems, Christians dare not isolate themselves from the world. The world is our objective, our target. It is the very thing we are here to reach. We dare not live out our Christian lives in air-tight compartments, limited only to Christian friends, in a sort of Christian hothouse.

The church exists on earth as God's instrument by which human life, in every area and at every level, is penetrated by the transforming gospel of Jesus Christ. The mission of the church is that men may see that Jesus Christ is the authentic voice of God to men, that in Him is the ultimate issue of human destiny, and in Him we come face to face with all that is important in human affairs.

This is a complex and painful problem, for we well know that, having once been on the other side of the fence, every worldling lives in confusion and blindness. He is suspicious and sensitive, especially about religious matters.

Today's worldling loves to remind us of what he considers a major rule of life: Never discuss politics or religion.

He may retreat under a hard shell of indifference and sophistication and seem unreachable. Yet that individual is our objective. Regardless of what attitudes or defenses we may encounter, our objective is to reach every man and woman, every boy and girl, giving each an opportunity to make an intelligent, informed choice to either accept or refuse Jesus Christ.

The Strategy

Now that we have identified the objective, what is our strategy? How does God plan to accomplish this? He has not given us the objective and left the strategy up to us. No, the strategy is found right here, in John 17, where Jesus prays for His disciples:

> "That all of them may be one, Father, just as you are in me and I am in you. May they also be in us so that the world may believe that you have sent me. I have given them the glory that you gave me, that they may be one as we are one: I in them and you in me. May they be brought to complete unity to let the world know that you sent me and have loved them even as you have loved me" (John 17:21–23).

Here is the strategy by which God intends to accomplish His objective: our oneness, our unity.

There are those who tell us that this prayer of Jesus concerning the church—"that they may be one"—must now begin to be answered. They believe that now—after twenty centuries of sectarian strife and schism and religious warfare—it is finally time for this prayer to be fulfilled. But is this prayer really unanswered today? Can it be possible for twenty centuries to roll by before God the Father would begin to fulfill this last request of Jesus? Is it possible that the World Council of Churches or some other ecumenical movement will finally succeed where God the Father has failed?

No. In truth, this prayer has been answered ever since the day of Pentecost. This strategy is not of human making. The business of making all Christians one does not depend upon us. It depends upon the Spirit of God. He came for that purpose. Paul's great chapter on the Holy Spirit in 1 Corinthians clearly establishes the fact that, in His coming, the Spirit accomplished precisely what Jesus prayed for. This is the divine strategy by which the world may be led to believe.

All Christians are one—not in union or in unison, but in a Spirit-endowed unity. There is a difference. Unison is an outward agreement. Union is an alliance or merger. But these are not unity. To speak in unison, various individuals have to deny their God-given individuality—they all have to sing one note. And to become a union, individual differences must be submerged so that all the individuals can be merged. It's easy to create unison or union—you don't need the Spirit to accomplish that. All you have to do is silence all the voices that sing a different note and you have unison. And all you have to do is kick out anyone who disagrees on any point, and those who are left have a union.

But unity is a different matter altogether. When Spirit-led Baptists and Spirit-led Pentecostals and Spirit-led Methodists and Spirit-led Catholics and Spirit-led Lutherans come together (and such things do happen, in settings ranging from small-group Bible studies to Promise Keepers rallies in football stadiums), there is unity. There may not be unison on doctrinal or denominational matters. There certainly is not union in organizational matters. But there is unity—a unity that is created by and maintained by the indwelling Spirit of God.

Every so often, we hear of two or three denominational groups that are holding talks and considering merging. Such mergers are neither automatically good nor bad—but they are artificial and organizational. Such mergers do not usually produce a more vibrant Christian witness in the world. More often, they simply produce larger, more monolithic power structures, which the worldlings resent as a threat to their own power structures. Such mergers do not answer the prayer of Jesus that we might all, as His disciples, be one. Such mergers do not convince the worldlings to believe that Jesus is the authentic voice of God. But the true oneness that comes from the Spirit does.

Some years ago, when I visited Taiwan, I was tremendously impressed by the remarkable oneness among the American missionaries, despite their denominational differences. At the great missionary conferences held once a year at Sun Moon Lake, high in the mountains of Taiwan, all the missionaries of the island—without exception, I believe—would gather together for a fellowship time. The denominations represented at these gatherings spanned the entire spectrum of Christianity, from the Mennonites to the more liberal churches and denominations. But what overwhelmingly impressed me was the glorious, heaven-like atmosphere of oneness that pervaded the entire group.

Some time later, an effort was made to join all the missionary groups in Taiwan into a single organization. What was the result? Factionalism broke out! They lost their wonderful unity!

Unity, as indicated in John 17, is not the merging of organizations but the sharing of a life: "That all of them may be one, Father, just as you are in me and I am in you" (verse 21). This is not alliance, nor merger, nor agreement; it is the sharing of life, which is quite a different matter. In the Lord's divine strategy, He intends to bring to the world a family life, a shared life, so that men and women all over the earth become members of that life by the new birth. As they become members of that life, they enter into a family circle so unmistakable and joyful that the worldlings will envy it. Like homeless orphans with their noses pressed up against the window, they will long to join the warmth and the fellowship of the family circle. When the church is like this, there is no evangelistic thrust more potent!

I once attended a men's retreat to which one man came who was evidently not yet a Christian. He was quite open about his agnosticism, and he told me he was embittered against the church, suspicious of the Scriptures, and committed in his life to habits not acceptable in Christian circles. He came with all his defenses and barriers raised. Yet the men accepted him where he was, and as the weekend went on, he could not resist the warmth of the Christian love expressed among those who were there. It was not surprising that by the end of the retreat, he too had joined the family circle of God. He could not stay away. He was won by our oneness.

That is the divine strategy—to make all Christians share one life in one great family. When the love-starved worldlings see our oneness, lived out in close and loving relationships in the church of Jesus Christ, they will want what we have.

And they will come to the One who makes us one.

The Glory is Love

Pastor-author Max Lucado has a simple but powerful way of demonstrating the power of the Person of Jesus Christ to unite people in His name. When he speaks to groups often numbering in the tens of thousands, there may be many individual churches and denominations represented. And Lucado will say, "On the count of three, I want you to shout out loud the name of the church or denomination you come from! One, two, three!" And the result is absolute cacophony and confusion—a meaningless roar of noise.

But then Lucado will go on to say, "Now, on the count of three, I want you to all shout the name of the One to whom you have committed your heart and soul and mind and strength. One, two, three!" The result is a stunning, resounding, unmistakably clear shout of "JESUS!" And always, after that shout, there is a stunned silence lasting several seconds—because those who are present suddenly realize how much they have in common in that one blessed Name. Denominations mean nothing, differences in doctrine or creed seem to vanish, as everyone who has just shouted that name realizes that he or she is gathered together in that Name, and that He is there in the midst of them, uniting their hearts, making them one in Him.

The life of Jesus Christ in the body of Christ is an invisible thing. That is why our unity is sometimes difficult to see. Something must make it visible—but what? Now we come to the divine tactics by which God intends to implement His strategy. What are His tactics? Jesus tells us in John 17:22:

> "I have given them the glory that you gave me, that they may be one as we are one."

The world will believe, He says, when it sees that the church is one. And what makes the church one? The glory that the Father has given Him, says Jesus. In verse 24, He goes on to say this about that glory:

"Father, I want those you have given me to be with me where I am, and to see my glory, the glory you have given me because you loved me before the creation of the world."

It is important to note that this is not a reference to glory at some far off future time in heaven, but a present glory, what Paul refers to in Ephesians when he says, "And God raised us up with Christ and seated us with him in the heavenly realms in Christ Jesus" (Ephesians 2:6). This is the glory of sharing what He is. Here is a glory, a flaming glory in the church which makes the unity of believers visible. What is it? Jesus is very specific: "I have made you known to them, and will continue to make you known in order that the love you have for me may be in them and that I myself may be in them" (verse 26).

The glory is love! In other words, the unity of the church is made visible when Christians love one another. That is the whole secret.

Now we have put our finger squarely on the reason for the failure of the church to reach the world in our day. Why are we seeing this remarkable upsurge of blatant attacks against the Christian faith? Why is there widespread apathy and outright hostility to biblical authority? Why have so many declared the voice of the church to be irrelevant to the times in which we live?

I don't believe it is only coincidence that recent decades have been largely characterized by church conflict, that during those years the world saw Christians hurling insults and accusations at one another, splitting theological hairs with ecclesiastical razor blades, then splitting over the splits! Some religious newspapers and magazines have been founded specifically in the cause of name-calling and heresy-hounding. They have devoted their energies to fighting one another rather than proclaiming the gospel of Jesus Christ. Is it any wonder that the world has turned a deaf ear to the church?

Charles Spurgeon spoke of people who go around with a theological revolver in their ecclesiastical holsters. We still have such gun-toting Christians with us today. That is why Jesus, when He gathered with His disciples in the Upper Room, left them this final word: "A new command I give you: Love one another. As I have loved you, so you must love one another" (John 13:34). Here is the key: Love one another. That is where world evangelization must start.

These are the tactics by which the divine strategy is implemented to reach the great objective, so that the world may believe that the Father has sent Jesus. That is why Jesus said, "By this all men will know that you are my disciples, if you love one another" (John 13:35). More than that, John says, "And he has given us this command: Whoever loves God must also love his brother" (1 John 4:21). It all begins with love. And this love is not to be mere sentiment, which has been described as "that warm feeling about the heart that you can't scratch." Nor is it something with which to disguise a dagger of dislike. The Scripture says, "Love must be sincere" (Romans 12:9).

There are three essential qualities to genuine Christian love. The first one is mutual contact. It is simply hogwash to speak of loving another Christian to whom you will not speak. There must be contact, the willingness to talk, with no aloofness, no withdrawal from each other. Now there are certain clearly described circumstances involving church discipline where Christians are to withdraw temporarily from one another, but those are very specific and only under unusual circumstances (see, for example, 1 Corinthians 5). But we are to love each other simply because we are Christians, and we are not to be selective about it.

It isn't only "our kind" of Christian, our specific group that we are to love—the ones that we feel something in common with. That kind of love is what the world employs. Jesus said, "And if you greet only your brothers, what are you doing more than others? Do not even pagans do that?" (Matthew 5:47). No, we are to love all of them simply because they are Christians, whether they are stupid or wrong or irritating or stubborn. Contact is first.

Second, genuine love involves mutual concern. By that I do not mean some superficial greeting in passing: "How are you today?" "Fine, just fine." Mutual concern means a willingness to genuinely share with each other and listen to each other. Every contact is to be marked by a readiness to help, to meet a need, to lend an ear, to pray—a willingness to bear one another's burdens in the Lord and so fulfill the law of Christ.

Third, all true Christian love is marked by a sense of mutual contribution. That means a recognition that we need each other, that we are not condescending when we give ourselves to another Christian. You have what another one needs, he has what you need, and we minister to one another, young and old alike. Some of the most helpful lessons I have ever learned have come to me from new babes in Christ with whom I have fellowshiped. They have taught me much. We need one another in the body of Christ.

It is significant that every great awakening throughout the whole course of Christian history has invariably begun by a breaking down of the barriers between Christians. When long-standing feuds have been resolved and apologies have been made; when pardons have been sought and confessions have been uttered; when barriers have been broken down by the irresistible force of Christlike love—the world sits up and takes notice of our message! That is love: contact, concern, contribution.

Let me add one thing more, because this love, as we recognize it so clearly in the Scriptures, is not something we work up from within. It is given to us by God. It is supernatural. It is in us by virtue of the fact that Jesus Christ is in us—but it does require our consent. The Lord is ready to love another Christian through us anytime we are ready to let ourselves be the channel of that love—and even if that Christian brother or sister is, to us in own human nature, unlovable. That is the whole position of Scripture. When we are ready to consent to love, He is quite ready to love through us.

What makes the Spirit heard and seen in His relentless quest to reach our blind, confused world is our willingness to be channels of His love to the world—glad to love any Christian, and glad to love any nonchristian into the Lord's kingdom.

I have resolved that my heart shall be always ready to love every person, without exception, in whom I sense a love for Jesus Christ, the Son of God, regardless of his denominational label or lack of it and despite any theological differences of viewpoint. I am ready, God in me and helping me, to give myself in love to any Christian, anywhere, whom I may chance to meet and in whom I sense a fellowship of love for Jesus Christ. That is the basis for Christian unity.

Are you willing to join in that commitment? Then pray this prayer with me: "Lord, in order to reach the world, I want you to teach me to give up my prejudices and sub-Christian attitudes toward my fellow brethren in Christ. Lord, make me willing to love them for Christ's sake." If you have prayed this most Christian of prayers, then I salute you as one who has entered the battle for the conquest of Planet Earth. You know the objective. You know the strategy. You know the tactics.

Now, go out today under that banner of King Jesus, and fight the battle of faith, the battle of prayer, the battle of love.

Father, you are the God of love. When we look at the cross of our Lord Jesus Christ, we see your love poured out for us. yours is a love that pursues us despite our rebuffs, a love that never gives up, a love that is relentless in its conquest of our hearts and souls. Thank you, Lord, for your relentless love.

Lord, we desire to live out this love that you have shown us. We ask that this love be shed abroad in our hearts by the Holy Spirit, who lives in us. We know that the world watches and waits to see this kind of love in Christian people. Father, there are so many people around us, in our neighborhoods and workplaces, people who hunger for your love. May we never dishonor your love, causing the worldlings around us to turn away in disappointment. Rather, let our lives shine with love before them, so that they will see where they can find your love for their own lives.

Lord, teach us then to love one another. Whatever this may mean in our day-to-day circumstances and relationships, teach us, Father, to love one another.

We pray this in Christ's name, Amen.

Note to the Reader

The publisher invites you to share your response to the message of this book by writing Discovery House Publishers, Box 3566, Grand Rapids, MI 49501, USA. For information about other Discovery House books, music, or videos, contact us at the same address or call 1-800-653-8333. Find us on the Internet at http://www.dhp.org/ or send e-mail to books@dhp.org.